Human Rights

Londo

Researched and written by Publishing Services, Central Office of Information

© Crown copyright 1995
Applications for reproduction should be made to HMSO Copyright Unit, St Crispins, Duke Street, Norwich NR3 1PD
First Edition Crown copyright 1992

ISBN 0 11 701593 8

Published by HMSO and available from:

HMSO Publications Centre
(Mail, fax and telephone orders only)
PO Box 276, London SW8 5DT
Telephone orders 0171 873 9090
General enquiries 0171 873 0011
(queuing system in operation for both numbers)
Fax orders 0171 873 8200

HMSO Bookshops
49 High Holborn, London WC1V 6HB
(counter service only)
0171 873 0011   Fax 0171 831 1326
68–69 Bull Street, Birmingham B4 6AD
0121 236 9696 Fax 0121 236 9699
33 Wine Street, Bristol BS1 2BQ
0117 9264306   Fax 0117 9294515
9–21 Princess Street, Manchester M60 8AS
0161 834 7201   Fax 0161 833 0634
16 Arthur Street, Belfast BT1 4GD
01232 238451   Fax 01232 235401
71 Lothian Road, Edinburgh EH3 9AZ
0131 228 4181   Fax 0131 229 2734
The HMSO Oriel Bookshop
The Friary, Cardiff CF1 4AA
01222 395548   Fax 01222 384347

HMSO's Accredited Agents
(see Yellow Pages)

and through good booksellers

Contents

Introduction	1
International Arrangements	2
British Institutions and Human Rights	11
Safeguarding Human Rights in Britain	13
Equal Opportunities	13
Protection of the Person	17
Equality Before the Law	23
Legal Procedure	31
Right to Privacy	37
Freedom of Movement	41
Political Asylum	42
Nationality	45
Marriage and the Family	47
Property	50
Religious Toleration	50
Freedom of Expression	53
Assemblies and Associations	58
Political Rights	59
Social Rights	66
Education, Science and the Arts	88
Safeguards for Human Rights	101
Texts of International Human Rights Documents	103
Further Reading	167
Index	170

Acknowledgments

The Central Office of Information would like to thank the following organisations for their co-operation in compiling this book: the Department for Education and Employment, the Department of the Environment, the Foreign & Commonwealth Office and the Home Office.

Cover Photograph Credit

Sally Greenhill.

Introduction

Great importance is attached in Britain[1] to human rights and the ways they are preserved and enlarged through the country's political and legal institutions. Respect for individual freedoms is embedded in British constitutional practice and forms a cornerstone of Britain's democratic system.

British public opinion is also concerned about violations of human rights throughout the world and the need for nations to observe international human rights standards agreed by the United Nations and other bodies. Britain, therefore, regards the observation of human rights and their protection as an important element of its foreign policy.

This book briefly describes international action designed to preserve human rights, including Britain's contribution. It also deals with some of the features of British political and legal institutions relevant to human rights. Using the 1948 Universal Declaration on Human Rights as a framework, it then outlines the steps taken to safeguard human rights in Britain.

---

[1] The term 'Britain' is used informally in this book to mean the United Kingdom of Great Britain and Northern Ireland; 'Great Britain' comprises England, Scotland and Wales.

International Arrangements

The twentieth century, having witnessed some of the most serious abuses of human rights in world history, has also seen a growing recognition that such abuses are the legitimate subject of international concern and that the promotion of human rights can no longer be left to national governments. International human rights standards have been set out in a series of international human rights instruments agreed by the United Nations,[2] the Council of Europe, the Organisation for Security and Co-operation in Europe (OSCE) and other bodies.

Some of these are legally binding on states which have ratified them, while others are declaratory and have only moral force. The elaboration of human rights law since 1945 now means that human rights violations can no longer be insulated from external criticism or expressions of concern on the grounds that the matter is exclusively a domestic one for the country concerned.

The British Government, therefore, believes that expressions of concern at violations of human rights cannot be considered as interference in a state's internal affairs. This principle was reaffirmed at the UN World Conference on Human Rights where Britain played a key part. It frequently raises human rights issues with other governments and acts with its European Union partners in joint protests about human rights violations. Other channels used are the United Nations and the OSCE. Bilateral action taken

[2] For more information see *Britain and the United Nations* (Aspects of Britain: HMSO, 1994).

by the British Government includes confidential representations, public statements, curtailment or reduction of aid, attending trials of dissidents, sending observers to elections and maintaining contacts with local human rights organisations under pressure from authoritarian governments and dictatorships.

United Nations

Under the UN Charter member states are pledged to promote and encourage respect for human rights and fundamental freedoms for all without distinction as to race, sex, language or religion. These rights and freedoms are listed in the Universal Declaration of Human Rights adopted by the UN General Assembly in 1948.

The Universal Declaration, however, is not a legally binding document. In 1966, therefore, the General Assembly adopted two international conventions placing legal obligations on those states ratifying or acceding to them. The covenants came into force in 1976, Britain ratifying both in the same year.

States parties to the International Covenant on Economic, Social and Cultural Rights (see pp. 103–15) are bound to promote the full realisation of these rights, which include the right to:

—work;

—an adequate standard of living;

—social security;

—education;

—the highest attainable health care standards;

—form and join trade unions; and

—participate in cultural life.

The Covenant's implementation is monitored by the UN Economic and Social Council. States parties submit reports on their implementation of the Covenant to the Committee on Economic, Social and Cultural Rights. The Committee considers the reports and then sends its findings to the UN Economic and Social Council which is formally charged with monitoring the implementation of the Covenant.

The International Covenant on Civil and Political Rights (see pp. 116–38) includes recognition of the right to:

—life;

—freedom from torture or cruel, inhuman or degrading treatment;

—freedom from slavery;

—freedom of movement;

—freedom from arbitrary expulsion;

—equality before the law;

—privacy;

—freedom of thought and religion;

—peaceful assembly;

—freedom of association, including trade union membership;

—take part in the conduct of public affairs;

—liberty; and

—freedom of expression.

Derogations from some of these obligations are permitted in time of an emergency threatening the life of a nation provided that these are justified by the situation. No derogation is permitted from certain articles such as those providing for the right to life, the prohibitions on torture and slavery and the right to freedom of thought, conscience or religion.

A Human Rights Committee monitors implementation of the Covenant's provisions. States parties to the Covenant are obliged to submit reports every five years on measures taken to give effect to these rights. The Committee may also consider communications from individuals claiming to be victims of violations where a state has accepted the Covenant's Optional Protocol.

Britain is also a party to a number of United Nations conventions designed to implement specific rights set out in the Universal Declaration. These include conventions on the:

—political rights of women;

—elimination of racial discrimination;

—status of refugees and stateless persons;

—prevention of torture;

—abolition of slavery and forced labour;

—prevention and punishment of genocide;

—right to organise and collective bargaining;

—freedom of association; and

—elimination of discrimination against women.

The Council of Europe

Britain is bound by the Council of Europe's European Convention for the Protection of Human Rights and Fundamental Freedoms (see pp. 144–61), which covers primarily civil and political rights. The main rights are:

—the right to life, liberty and a fair trial;

—freedom of thought, conscience and religion;

—freedom of expression, including freedom of the press;

—freedom of peaceful assembly and association, including the right to join a free trade union;

—the right to justice, including the right to have a sentence reviewed by a higher tribunal;

—the right to marry and have a family; and

—the prohibition of torture and inhuman or degrading treatment.

There are 11 Protocols to the Convention, three of which contain further rights (numbers 1, 4 and 6). Britain is a party to the First Protocol, which covers rights concerning the peaceful enjoyment of possessions; education; and free elections. Britain is not a party to the Fourth Protocol (on freedom of movement) because of inconsistency with some aspects of the country's immigration control system nor to the Sixth Protocol (abolition of the death penalty) for constitutional reasons.

The Convention recognises that some restrictions on these rights may be necessary on grounds of national security or the prevention of crime. It also permits states to suspend certain of their obligations in time of war or other public emergencies. No state can avoid its obligation to respect the right to life and to prohibit torture and slavery.

Enforcement of the Convention

Under the Convention, which came into force in 1953, one member state can complain about alleged breaches of the Convention by another. There is also a right of individual petition against governments to the European Commission of Human Rights, which decides whether cases meet the various conditions governing admissibility; applicants must show that they have exhausted all possible domestic remedies.

Once it is decided that an application is admissible, the Commission tries to achieve a friendly settlement between the parties. If no solution is found, it reports the matter to the Committee of Ministers, which consists of foreign ministers or their deputies from the member states. The issue can then be referred by the Commission or the state concerned to the European Court of Human Rights, provided that the state against which the case has been brought accepts the Court's jurisdiction. The Court rules on whether there has been a breach of the Convention and may award compensation to an individual complainant.

If the case is not referred to the Court within three months, the Committee of Ministers decides whether a breach has occurred. The Committee oversees the execution of both types of judgment. Britain has ratified a new protocol which will replace the existing Commission and Court with a full-time Court.

Since 1966 Britain has accepted the right of individual petition under the Convention and the compulsory jurisdiction of the Court. The outcome of some cases has led to changes in British law to improve human rights, for example the abolition of corporal punishment in state schools and improved rights for prisoners.

In recent years considerable debate has taken place in Britain about incorporating the European Convention into British law. The supporters of such a change argue that at present the freedoms granted by the Convention cannot be invoked directly before the British courts and that the procedure of petitioning the European Commission on Human Rights can be long and expensive. The Government, on the other hand, believes that this would involve the judges directly in areas of political controversy and that human rights are best secured through access to an independent and impartial judiciary.

The Organisation for Security and Co-operation in Europe

There are now 53 members of the Organisation for Security and Co-operation in Europe (OSCE), including most of the countries in Europe, the states of the former Soviet Union, and the United States and Canada. Until 1994 the OSCE was called the Conference on Security and Co-operation in Europe (CSCE). At that conference, held in Helsinki in 1975, Britain and other participants signed the Final Act which contains commitments to respect human rights and fundamental freedoms and to encourage 'the effective exercise of civil, economic, social, cultural and other rights and freedoms'.

In 1989 the Helsinki Final Act signatories agreed to create machinery allowing them to raise human rights issues with the other participants. Under this, a signatory can request information from another on human rights cases or situations. A state can also bring cases to the attention of the other participating states. These arrangements were strengthened in 1990, when states agreed to provide written responses to written requests for information within four weeks and to meet requests for bilateral meetings within three weeks.

At their Paris meeting in November 1990 CSCE leaders adopted and signed the Charter of Paris for a New Europe, which gives clearer expression to the human rights and freedoms which must be preserved in a democratic society based on the rule of law (see pp. 162-3). It also stresses the need to protect the rights of national minorities and identifies the freedom of the individual as the basis for successful economic and social development.

The European Union

As part of their political co-operation on foreign policy, Britain[3] and the other 14 European Union member states have consistently reaffirmed the importance of protecting human rights throughout the world. This policy was set out in a declaration adopted in 1986 which said: 'The protection of human rights is the legitimate and continuous duty of the world community and of nations individually. Expressions of concern at violations of such rights cannot be considered interference in the domestic affairs of a state.' In 1991 the European Council adopted a new declaration reaffirming member states' commitment to the promotion of human rights.

Action taken by the 15 member states includes declarations, representations to governments, the adoption of common positions at the United Nations and other international forums and co-ordinated diplomatic pressure on a government.

The Commonwealth

Commonwealth[4] heads of Government have issued declarations reaffirming the importance they attach to human rights. At their meeting in Harare in 1991 they reaffirmed their strong collective commitment to the principles of justice and human rights, including the rule of law, the independence of the judiciary, equality for women and accountable administrations; they also requested the Commonwealth Secretariat to give greater impetus to the

[3] For further information see the following titles in the Aspects of Britain series: *European Union* (HMSO, 1994) and *Britain in the European Community* (HMSO, 1992).

[4] For further information see *Britain and the Commonwealth* (Aspects of Britain: HMSO, 1992).

promotion of human rights (see pp. 164-6). Britain wants the Commonwealth to increase its understanding of the major international human rights instruments and to encourage their ratification by all Commonwealth countries. The Secretariat's Human Rights Unit promotes understanding and respect for human rights throughout the Commonwealth.

Aid and Human Rights

The Government attempts to promote good government through its aid programme to developing countries. Good government includes:

—sound economic and social policies;

—effective, open and accountable institutions; and

—respect for human rights and the rule of law.

In Britain's view, democracy and respect for human rights reinforce sound economic policies and produce conditions in which individual initiative can flourish. Aid is used in a practical way to support economic and social reform, increase the effectiveness of governments and help strengthen democratic institutions such as a free press, an independent judiciary and free elections.

British Institutions and Human Rights

The British legal systems[5] provide a number of remedies to deal with human rights abuses. In England, Wales and Northern Ireland, for instance, the remedy of 'habeas corpus' secures the individual's right to freedom from any unlawful or arbitrary detention. An individual can also bring a court action against false imprisonment. These rights are guaranteed by the judicial system which is strictly independent of the executive.

In addition to legal remedies, the citizen can obtain impartial scrutiny of action by public bodies if he or she feels that there is cause for complaint (see p. 24).

There are also some non-legal safeguards against the abuse of government power, including unwritten parliamentary conventions, the vigilance of parliamentary opposition parties and of Members of Parliament (MPs), the influence of a free press and public opinion, and the right to change the Government through free elections by secret ballot.

When considering the preservation and extension of human rights in Britain, several features of the system of government need to be borne in mind:

—Parliament has power to enact any law and change any previous law. Because of Britain's membership of the European Union,

---

[5] For further information see the following titles in the Aspects of Britain series: *Britain's Legal Systems* (HMSO, 1993) and *Criminal Justice* (HMSO, 1995).

Community law is part of British law and takes precedence in the event of conflict between the two.

— There is no written constitution or comprehensive Bill of Rights. Britain's constitution is to be found partly in conventions and customs and partly in statute. The Act known as the Bill of Rights 1689 deals with the exercise of the royal prerogative and succession to the Crown.

— There is no fundamental distinction in English or Scots law between 'public law', governing the relationship between the State and the individual, and 'private law', governing the relationship between individuals. Any person can take proceedings against the Government or a local government authority to protect his or her legal rights and to obtain a remedy for any injury suffered.

— Britain has not generally codified its law and courts adopt a relatively strict and literal approach to the interpretation of statutes.

— The ratification of a treaty or international convention does not make it automatically part of domestic law. Where necessary, the Government amends domestic law to bring it in line with the convention concerned.

Safeguarding Human Rights in Britain

In the following pages the UN Universal Declaration of Human Rights is used to show how human rights are protected in Britain. Article 1 states that 'all human beings are born free and equal in dignity and rights ... endowed with reason and conscience and should act towards one another in a spirit of brotherhood'.

Equal Opportunities

Article 2. Everyone is entitled to all the rights and freedoms set forth in this Declaration without distinction of any kind, such as race, colour, sex, language, religion, political or other opinion, national or social origin, property, birth or other status.

Legislation bans discrimination on grounds of sex or ethnic origin in a wide number of areas. In Northern Ireland legislation deals with discrimination on grounds of religious belief or political opinion.

Sex Discrimination

It is unlawful to treat one person less favourably than another on grounds of sex[6] in employment, education, training and the provision of housing, goods, facilities and services such as insurance. Advertisements indicating an intention to discriminate in job recruitment are also illegal.

[6] For further information see *Women in Britain* (Aspects of Britain: HMSO, 1996).

Complaints about discrimination are heard by a civil court of law or, in employment cases, an industrial tribunal. Complainants can be represented by a lawyer. If the court or the tribunal decides that discrimination has taken place, remedies include compensation or damages, a declaration of rights or an order to carry out, or refrain from, specified acts. There is a right of appeal against a court or tribunal decisions.

Equal Pay

Women employed by the same employer can claim the same pay as men for work of equal value. This right also applies to work which is the same or broadly similar or work which is judged equal by a job evaluation scheme. The same rights apply to men. Industrial tribunals decide disputed cases. Legislation on equal pay was extended to meet European Union requirements by providing for equal pay for work of equal value.

Equal Opportunities Commission

The Equal Opportunities Commission helps to enforce the legislation, promotes equality of opportunity between men and women and provides advice and financial and other assistance to help people conduct a case before a court or tribunal. The Commission is the only body allowed to take legal action against discriminatory advertisements, instructions to discriminate or persistent discrimination. It can also conduct formal investigations and issue notices requiring discriminatory practices to stop. The Equal Opportunities Commission for Northern Ireland has similar functions.

European Community Legislation

Under European Community legislation, member states are obliged to eliminate discrimination in state social security schemes providing protection against sickness, unemployment, invalidity, old age, accidents at work or occupational diseases. There are, however, some exclusions such as pensionable age. Britain has implemented this legislation.

Racial Equality

The Government believes that all people in a multi-racial society should have the same rights and responsibilities.[7] Under legislation passed in 1976 it is unlawful to treat one person less favourably than another on grounds of race, colour, nationality or ethnic or national origins. This applies to the provision to the public of goods, facilities and services, employment (including training), housing, education and advertising. Complaints of racial discrimination are heard by the civil courts and, for employment complainants, industrial tribunals. Although there is at present no legislation on race relations in Northern Ireland, the Government intends to introduce legislation on the lines of the Race Relations Act 1976. It is also, in the context of the peace process in Northern Ireland, considering how civil, political and cultural rights might be further protected in the province.

Commission for Racial Equality

The Commission for Racial Equality helps enforce the legislation. It has the power to assist individuals to bring complaints before the courts and industrial tribunals and is solely responsible for bringing proceedings regarding discriminatory practices, advertisements and pressure to discriminate. It also has powers to deal with persistent discrimination. In addition, it can conduct formal

[7] For further information see *Ethnic Minorities* (Aspects of Britain: HMSO, 1991).

investigations; if it finds that the legislation has been contravened, it can issue a non-discrimination notice which is enforceable in the courts by an injunction or court order.

The Commission has issued codes of practice in employment, education, health care, maternity services and housing.

Northern Ireland

Direct and indirect discrimination in employment on grounds of religious belief or political opinion is against the law in Northern Ireland. All public authorities and all private sector employers with more than ten employees must register with the Fair Employment Commission and submit annual returns to it on the religious composition of their workforces. Failure to do so is a criminal offence and may render the employer liable to economic sanctions, such as exclusion from government contracts or grants.

The Fair Employment Commission has power to direct an employer to take affirmative action, such as the encouragement of job applications from an under-represented group. It can also set goals and timetables in cases where fair participation by both sides of the Northern Ireland community in employment is not being afforded. The Commission has published a code of practice setting out detailed recommendations for employers and others on the promotion of equality of opportunity.

The Fair Employment Tribunal adjudicates on individual complaints of discrimination and may award damages and order remedial action by an employer. It also has powers to enforce directions made by the Commission.

In line with a commitment made by the Government, a major review of the legislation is under way. The results are expected to be published towards the end of 1996. The review is being undertaken by the independent Standing Advisory Commission for Human Rights, which advises the Government on the adequacy and effectiveness of anti-discrimination laws.

Protection of the Person

Article 3. Everyone has the right to life, liberty and the security of person.

Taking of Life

The deliberate taking of life is a criminal offence. The mandatory penalty for murder is imprisonment for life. Anyone sent to prison for murder is liable to be detained for the rest of his or her life but may be released on licence (see p. 22).

Control of Firearms

There is strict licensing and control over the sale of firearms and their possession in order to minimise the risk of injury and loss of life through their use. The police have powers to regulate the possession, safekeeping and movement of firearms and shotguns. The private ownership of certain highly dangerous types of weapons such as machine guns and high-powered self-loading rifles is banned. Owners of firearms and shotguns must have a certificate issued by the police. The maximum sentence for carrying firearms while engaged in crime is life imprisonment.

The police in England, Scotland and Wales do not normally carry firearms, although they can be issued in an emergency on the authority of a senior officer.

Violence to the Person

Any deliberate violence directed against other people is a criminal offence. In addition to any penalty imposed upon a convicted criminal, a court can grant a compensation order against a criminal which takes precedence over a fine. If compensation is not awarded by the court, reasons must be given for not granting it. Under the civil law financial damages can be recovered for any assault.

Victims of violent crime, including foreign nationals, may apply for compensation under the Criminal Injuries Compensation Scheme.

In Northern Ireland there is statutory compensation in certain circumstances for criminal injuries and for malicious damage to property, including the resulting loss of profits.

There are about 370 victim support schemes with trained volunteers, providing practical help and emotional support to victims of crime. Covering 98 per cent of the population in England and Wales, these schemes are co-ordinated by a national organisation, Victim Support, which receives a government grant (£10.8 million in 1995–96). There are similar schemes in Scotland and Northern Ireland.

In England and Wales a publicly funded witness service provides support for victims and other witnesses attending Crown Courts.

Emergency Legislation (Northern Ireland)
In order to protect the public, the Northern Ireland (Emergency Provisions) Act 1991 gives the authorities exceptional powers to deal with and prevent terrorist activities. Designed to achieve a proper balance between public safety and assuring the rights of the individual, it is subject to annual independent review and to annual approval by Parliament. Although ceasefires have been implemented by republican and loyalist terrorists, the legislation is in force, pending a political settlement (see p. 62). The 1991 Act

reaches the end of its life in August 1996. The Government hopes that, once a lasting peace is established, there will be no need for these exceptional powers. It is, therefore, keeping the requirement for such powers under continuing review.

The security forces have special powers to question and arrest people suspected of being involved in terrorism and to search property, including vehicles. It is an offence to be a member of a terrorist organisation or to demonstrate support for terrorism. It is a crime to take part in racketeering organised by terrorists, and proceeds arising from such crime can be confiscated by the courts.

Terrorist suspects can be detained for questioning for up to seven days. A suspect can be detained longer than 48 hours only with the written authority of the Northern Ireland Secretary. After seven days the person must be either charged and brought before a court or released.

Incitement to Racial Hatred

Incitement to racial hatred is a criminal offence. It is against the law to use threatening, abusive or insulting words or to display, publish or distribute such material. It is also an offence to possess inflammatory material, the police having powers of search, seizure and forfeiture. Several initiatives have been established that are designed to tackle racially motivated crimes and to ensure that these are treated by the police as a priority.

Northern Ireland legislation prohibits the use of written matter or words likely to, or intended to, provoke hatred based on religious belief, colour, race or ethnic or national origin.

Article 4. No one shall be held in slavery or servitude; slavery and the slave trade shall be prohibited in all their forms.

Slavery ceased to exist in the British Isles many centuries ago and Britain took the lead in the abolition of the slave trade throughout the world. In 1834 slavery was abolished in British possessions in all parts of the world.

Article 5. No one shall be subjected to torture or to cruel, inhuman or degrading treatment or punishment.

Protection for Accused People

Under a government code of practice, a police officer in England and Wales or Northern Ireland must not try to obtain admissions from an arrested person by oppression. If a police officer fails to comply with these provisions, he or she can be disciplined and the courts may reject any evidence so obtained.

In Scotland the courts reject statements made by an accused person unless satisfied that they have been fairly obtained.

Use of Custody

Under the Criminal Justice Act 1991, a custodial sentence in England and Wales can be imposed only where the offence is so serious that only such a sentence would be appropriate, or where there is a need to protect the public from a sexual or violent offender. The court is required to explain to the offender why it is passing a custodial sentence. The length of the sentence must reflect the seriousness of the offence, although longer sentences—within the statutory maxima—may be imposed on violent and sexual offenders.

Non-custodial Treatment

The Government takes the view that, while those convicted of serious crimes should be given long sentences, lesser crimes such as against property should be punished in the community by means of fines, compensation to the victim, probation, community service or a mixture of probation and community service.

About 80 per cent of offenders are punished with a fine. Probation involves the supervision of offenders in the community; this is intended as a punishment but offers an opportunity for constructive work to reduce the likelihood of reoffending. Other offenders are sentenced to compulsory community service, for example decorating the houses of elderly or disabled people or building adventure playgrounds for young children. All community service schemes have to meet national standards.

Early Release of Prisoners

Prisoners serving terms of less than four years may be released after half of their sentence; remission for longer-term prisoners is two-thirds. All prisoners may be supervised on release until three-quarters of their sentence is passed. Some sexual offenders may be supervised to the end of their sentence.

In Northern Ireland remission is half the sentence if it is more than five days; a prisoner serving more than 12 months can be ordered to serve the remainder of the sentence if convicted of fresh offences during the remitted period. Remission for those convicted of terrorist offences and serving sentences of five years or more is one-third.

Parole

Under the Criminal Justice Act 1991 parole in England and Wales can be given for prisoners half-way through sentences if they are serving between four and seven years. Parole for longer-term prisoners (serving more than seven years) may be granted only after the consent of the Home Secretary.

If convicted of another offence punishable with imprisonment and committed before the end of the original sentence, a released prisoner may be liable to serve all or part of the original sentence outstanding at the time the fresh offence was committed.

Similar arrangements are now in use in Scotland.

Life Sentence Prisoners

The Home Secretary or the Secretary of State for Scotland is required to release prisoners serving life sentences other than murder after a period set by the trial judge if so directed by the Parole Board, which has to be satisfied that the protection of the public does not need their further imprisonment.

The release on licence of prisoners serving mandatory life sentences for murder may only be authorised by the Home Secretary on the recommendation of the Parole Board. Similar policy applies in Scotland.

Life sentence prisoners are released on life licence and are subject to recall should their behaviour suggest that they might again be a danger to the public.

People serving life sentences for the murder of police or prison officers, terrorist murders, murder by firearms in the course of robbery and the sexual or sadistic murder of children are normally detained for at least 20 years.

In Northern Ireland the Secretary of State reviews life sentence cases on the recommendation of an internal review body.

Council of Europe Convention

Prisoners who are nationals of countries which have ratified the Council of Europe's Convention on the Transfer of Sentenced Persons may apply to be returned to their own country to serve the rest of their sentence there.

Equality Before the Law

Article 6. Everyone has the right to recognition everywhere as a person before the law.

Article 7. All are equal before the law and are entitled without any discrimination to equal protection of the law. All are entitled to equal protection against any discrimination in violation of this Declaration and against any incitement to such discrimination.

Article 8. Everyone has the right to an effective remedy by the competent national tribunals for acts violating the fundamental rights granted him by the constitution or by the law.

Legal Redress and Remedies

The courts are one of the chief ways by which people can be protected against abuses of their human rights. Everyone has the right of access to the courts and to the legal remedies available there.

Effective remedies are proceedings before the criminal courts which may result in the conviction of the offender or a civil court action which may result in the award of damages. Other civil redress may include a court order against the wrongdoer; if the order is not observed, the person refusing to obey can be imprisoned, fined or have his or her property sequestrated.

In Wales, anyone wishing to speak Welsh in any legal proceedings is free to do so.

Legal Aid

Legal aid schemes help people with limited resources to meet the cost of work done by a lawyer. This includes advice and assistance and, if there is a reasonable case, aid in criminal and civil proceedings. People receiving help may be required—according to their means—to pay a contribution. In some urban areas law centres provide free advice to people of limited means. Free legal advice is also obtainable from independent Citizens Advice Bureaux.

Solicitors give legal advice and assistance to suspects at police stations.

Judicial Control of Public Authorities

All state authorities are subject to judicial control, with the exception of Parliament as a whole and any subordinate body whose decisions have been expressly excluded by Parliament from review by the courts. Government departments and public authorities can be sued for compensation for wrongful acts or breach of contract in the same way as individuals.

Maladministration

Members of the public have the right to make a complaint if they think they have suffered injustice as a result of maladministration by a government department or by the staff of courts and tribunals administered by the Lord Chancellor's Department. The complaint has to be made through the complainant's MP to the Parliamentary Commissioner for Administration (the Parliamentary Ombudsman), who has the power to conduct an investigation. This may involve the examination of records and the questioning of ministers and civil servants. The Ombudsman reports the results of the investigation to the MP who raised the grievance. Where maladministration is established, various financial remedies can be applied. Most of the Ombudsman's recommendations are put into practice. An annual report is made to Parliament; selected cases are published three times a year.

The Ombudsman also monitors a code of practice on open government (see p.66), investigating complaints that government departments or bodies have refused to give official information.

There is also complaints machinery covering maladministration in local government and the National Health Service.

Northern Ireland has its own Complaints Commissioner, whose recommendations are legally enforceable.

Complaints against the Police

In England and Wales the independent Police Complaints Authority has power to supervise the investigation of any serious complaint against a police officer. It also reviews the reports of every investigation, whether supervised or not, to decide whether disciplinary charges should be made against the officer who is the subject of the complaint. Investigations are carried out by the police.

There is a separate Independent Commission for Police Complaints in Northern Ireland.

In Scotland complaints against police officers involving allegations of any form of criminal conduct are investigated by independent prosecutors. The Scottish Inspectorate of Constabulary deals with the handling of a complaint where a complainant is dissatisfied.

Article 9. No one shall be subjected to arbitrary arrest, detention or exile.

Everyone has a legal right to personal liberty. No one can be arrested except those suspected of committing a crime, those failing to comply with certain civil court orders or individuals in contempt of a superior court or of Parliament. An arrest to enforce a court order in civil proceedings can only be made under a warrant issued by a court or by a power of arrest granted by the court in cases of domestic violence.

Arrests in Criminal Proceedings

In England and Wales the police have the power to arrest without warrant anyone suspected of having committed an arrestable offence. Normally this is an offence for which the sentence is fixed by law or carries a term of imprisonment of five years or more. The police also have a power of general arrest for lesser offences if, for example, they are unable to obtain a satisfactory name and address for the service of a summons or the officer believes it is necessary to arrest the person to prevent further injury or damage. A police officer may also arrest a person in the execution of a warrant issued by a magistrate.

In Scotland a warrant is issued by a sheriff at the request of the public prosecutor where there is enough information to charge a person with a crime meriting trial by jury. In addition, decisions of the courts have established police powers at common law to arrest a suspect without warrant for any offence if it is in the interests of justice to do so, for example, to prevent the suspect from committing further offences or absconding. A person can also be searched for stolen property if the police have reasonable grounds for suspicion.

Rights of Arrested People

Contacts between the police in the exercise of their powers and the public are contained in Codes of Practice approved by Parliament. The Codes regulate police powers and procedures in the investigation of crime and set down safeguards and protections for members of the public. Failure to comply with the Codes' provisions can render a police officer liable to disciplinary proceedings. Evidence obtained in breach of the code may be ruled inadmissible in court.

An arrested person has the right to:

—consult a solicitor;

—ask the police to notify a relative or other named person likely to take an interest in his or her welfare; and

—consult the code of practice regarding treatment in police custody.

The policy may delay the exercise of the first two of these rights for up to 36 hours in the interests of the investigation if certain criteria are met and the suspect has been arrested in connection with a serious arrestable offence such as murder.

Solicitors are available on a 24-hour basis to offer free legal advice for people being questioned at police stations.

A suspect may refuse to answer police questions or to give evidence in court. Changes to this so-called 'right to silence' were made by the Criminal Justice and Public Order Act 1994 to allow courts to draw inferences from a defendant's refusal to answer police questions or to give information during his or her trial. Reflecting this change in the law, a new form of police caution (which must precede any questions to a suspect for the purpose of obtaining evidence) is intended to ensure that people understand the possible consequences if they answer questions or stay silent.

The length of time a suspect is held by the police is strictly regulated. The suspect may not normally be detained for more than 24 hours without charge. A person suspected of committing a serious arrestable offence, however, may be detained for up to 36 hours without charge on the authority of a senior police officer; if the police wish to detain the suspect for longer than 36 hours, they must obtain authority from a court, which may not grant authority for a period beyond 96 hours from the start of detention.

Reviews must be made of a person's detention at regular intervals to check whether the criteria for detention are still satisfied. If they are not, the person must be released immediately.

In any period of 24 hours a detained person must be allowed a continuous period of at least eight hours for rest, free from questioning, travel or other interruption arising from the investigation. Police cells must be adequately lit, heated, cleaned and ventilated. Access to toilet and washing facilities must be provided, as well as suitable food and clothing.

The tape recording of interviews with suspected offenders at police stations is now virtually universal in England and Wales. A code of practice regarding these tape recordings has been approved by Parliament.

The Government is extending police powers to take non-intimate body samples without consent from suspects. The police would be able to use the samples to search against existing records of convicted offenders or unsolved crimes.

In almost all areas in England, Wales and Northern Ireland lay visitors are allowed to check on the treatment of people detained in police stations.

In Scotland the police may detain and question a suspect for up to six hours; at the end of this period the suspect must be either released or charged.

A person who thinks that the grounds for detention are unlawful may apply to the High Court for a writ of habeas corpus against the person detaining him or her. If no lawful cause can be shown, the person must be released immediately. A habeas corpus case has priority over other cases in the order of court business. In Scotland a similar remedy is available to anyone who is unlawfully detained.

Charging

Once there is sufficient evidence for a charge, the police have to decide whether or not to charge a person with the offence. As an alternative to charging immediately, they can decide to defer charging or take no further action. They may issue a caution, which is a warning that prosecution is likely for a second offence.

When a suspect is charged, the person may be kept in custody if there is a risk that he or she might fail to appear in court or may interfere with the course of justice. A young person may also be detained for his or her protection. When no such considerations apply, the person must be released on or without bail. Where someone is detained after charge, he or she must be brought before a court quickly. This will usually be no later than the next working day.

Bail

Most accused people are released by the court on bail pending trial. Unconditional bail may be withheld only if the court has substantial grounds for believing that the accused would:

—abscond;

—commit an offence;

—interfere with witnesses; or

—otherwise obstruct the course of justice.

In such circumstances the accused can be remanded in custody by the court.

A court may impose conditions before granting bail. If bail is refused, the defendant may apply to a High Court judge or to the Crown Court for bail. In Scotland the accused may apply to the court that made the original decision and has the right of appeal to the High Court of Justiciary.

In some cases a court may grant bail to a defendant on condition that he or she lives in an approved bail or probation/bail hostel.

To stop people reoffending while on bail, new legislation gives the police powers of immediate arrest and removes the presumption in favour of bail for people alleged to have offended while on bail.

Time Limits on Remands in Custody

There are time limits on the period a defendant may be held in custody awaiting trial in England and Wales. In cases tried by the magistrates' court these are 56 days from first appearance to trial by them or 70 days between first appearance in a magistrates' court to committal for trial in the Crown Court. The limit in the Crown Court, which tries people charged with more serious offences, is 112 days from committal to taking of the plea. When a limit expires, the defendant is entitled to bail unless the court extends the limit; it can do this only if satisfied that the prosecution has acted expeditiously.

In Scotland the trial must begin within 110 days of the date of full committal if a person is to be prosecuted on indictment for a serious offence and is kept in custody awaiting trial. The trial of a person charged with a less serious offence (a summary offence) and held in custody must begin within 40 days.

Prosecution

Once the police have charged a person with a crime, the Crown Prosecution Service (CPS) in England and Wales takes control over the case, reviews the evidence and decides whether to prosecute. Decisions are reached by applying two criteria—the evidential test and the public interest test—which are set in the code for Crown Prosecutors. Crown Prosecutors must be satisfied that there is enough evidence to provide 'a realistic prospect of conviction' against each defendant on each charge, and that the evidence can be used and is reliable. Having satisfied himself or herself that the evidence can justify proceedings, the Crown Prosecutor must then consider whether the public interest requires a prosecution. Only cases which meet both these criteria should be prosecuted.

The CPS provides prosecution lawyers for the magistrates' courts and briefs barristers to appear in the Crown Court.

In Scotland, public prosecutors decide whether or not to bring proceedings and in Northern Ireland the decision is made by the Director of Public Prosecutions.

Legal Procedure

Article 10. Everyone is entitled in full equality to a fair and public hearing by an independent and impartial tribunal in the determination of his rights and obligations and of any criminal charge against him.

Civil and criminal cases are heard by an independent judiciary. The Government cannot force judges to act in a partial manner nor delay the course of justice. Both parties in a trial have the right to an independent judge, to be heard and to be represented by a lawyer. In criminal cases the prosecution must prove guilt beyond reasonable doubt. The standard of proof required in civil court actions is lower than in a criminal case.

The Courts

Most criminal charges (the less serious) are dealt with by lay magistrates' courts in England, Wales and Northern Ireland. These sit without a jury. In Scotland minor offences are considered by non-jury district courts and less serious ones by the sheriff court sitting without a jury; more serious sheriff court cases are tried by jury. Serious offences such as murder, armed robbery and rape are tried in higher courts—the Crown Court in England, Wales and Northern Ireland and the High Court of Justiciary in Scotland—which sit with a jury.

In Northern Ireland trial by jury for terrorist-type offences has been abolished because of the possibility of intimidation of jurors and the danger of perverse verdicts. The onus, however, remains on the prosecution to prove guilt beyond reasonable doubt and accused people have the right to legal representation. If the judge convicts the defendant, the reasons for convicting must be set out in a written statement. There is an automatic right of appeal against conviction or sentence.

The Jury

In jury trials the judge decides questions of law, sums up the evidence for the jury and discharges the accused or passes sentence. In England, Wales and Northern Ireland the jury is responsible for deciding whether the defendant is 'guilty' or 'not guilty', the latter verdict resulting in acquittal. If the jury cannot reach a unanimous decision, the judge allow a majority verdict provided that there are not more than two dissenters in a jury of 12 people.

In Scotland the jury's verdict may be 'guilty', 'not guilty' or 'non proven'; the accused is acquitted if either of the last two verdicts is given. The jury consists of 15 people. A 'guilty' verdict can be reached only if at least eight members are in favour. No one can be convicted, except where legislation directs otherwise, without corroborated evidence from at least two sources.

A jury is independent of the judiciary. Any attempt to interfere with the jury once it is sworn in is a criminal offence.

The jury consists of independent citizens chosen at random from the electoral register. Potential jurors are put on a panel before the start of the trial. In England and Wales the prosecution and the defence may challenge individual jurors on the panel, provided that they give reasons for doing so. In Scotland the prosecution or defence may challenge up to three jurors without putting forward a reason. In Northern Ireland the defendant can challenge up to 12 potential jurors without giving a reason.

Anyone who has received a prison sentence of five years or more is disqualified for life from jury service. Other disqualifications include:

—people who have served certain custodial sentences within the previous ten years;

—people who have received a community service order within the previous ten years;

—anyone who has been placed on probation within the previous five years; and

—people on bail.

Other ineligible people include judges, clergy and those who have within the previous ten years been members of the legal profession or the police, prison or probation services.

The Courts and the Media

Court proceedings are normally held in public and reporters from the media are admitted. Certain restrictions may, however, be placed on media reporting to protect children in criminal and civil proceedings and to preserve the more intimate details of the private lives of the parties to domestic and matrimonial proceedings. In rape cases, for instance, the identity of the complainant cannot be reported.

In England and Wales there are also restrictions on court reporting where magistrates make preliminary enquiries into a more serious case to see whether there is enough evidence to justify trial by jury in a higher court. Reports on such proceedings are limited to identification of the people concerned, descriptions of the offence or offences being enquired into and the recording of the court's decisions. The evidence must not be reported except at the defendant's request unless the latter is discharged by the magistrates.

Comment as well as factual reporting by the media on civil or criminal trials is allowed provided that it does not seriously impair or prejudice the course of justice.

Administrative Tribunals

In addition to the civil and criminal courts, there are administrative tribunals which decide disputes between private citizens or resolve claims by individuals against public authorities. Others, including tax tribunals, decide disputed claims by public authorities against private citizens.

The powers, functions and procedures of tribunals are settled by Parliament. There is a right of appeal, on a point of law, from the more important tribunals to a court of law. In other cases appeals may be made to a special appeal tribunal, to a government minister or to an independent referee. The Council on Tribunals and its Scottish committee supervise the constitution and working of most tribunals.

Criminal Trials

Article 11. (i) Everyone charged with a penal offence has the right to be presumed innocent until proved guilty

according to law in a public trial at which he has had all the guarantees necessary for his defence.

(ii) No one shall be held guilty of any penal offence on account of any act or omission which did not constitute a penal offence, under national or international law, at the time when it was committed. Nor shall a heavier penalty be imposed than the one that was applicable at the time the penal offence was committed.

Criminal trials in Britain have two parties—the prosecution and the defence. Since the law presumes the innocence of an accused person until guilt has been proved, the prosecution is not granted any advantage over the defence.

Rights of the Defence
A defendant has the right to employ a legal adviser and may be granted legal aid from public funds to help pay his or her costs. If remanded in custody, he or she may be visited by a legal adviser to ensure a properly prepared defence.

It is for the prosecution to prove that the defendant committed the crime alleged. In order for the defendant to understand the nature of the case against him or her, the defence must be informed of all the relevant information that the prosecution has, whether or not it forms part of its case.

Where cases are to be tried in the Crown Court, the CPS must also disclose to the defence at an early stage all the statements from the prosecution witnesses upon whom it proposes to rely. This duty does not apply to offences tried in the magistrates' court, except when advance information is requested by the defence in those cases which could be tried either by magistrates or in the Crown Court.

In Scotland the prosecution must give the defence advance notice of the witnesses it will call.

During the trial the defendant has the right to hear and cross-examine prosecution witnesses, normally through a lawyer. He or she can call his or her own witnesses, who may be legally compelled to attend if they will not do so voluntarily. The defendant can also address the court in person or through a lawyer, the defence having the last word at the trial before the judge sums up the evidence. The defendant cannot be questioned without consenting to be sworn as a witness in his or her own defence. If he or she does decide to testify, cross-examination about character or other conduct may be made only in exceptional circumstances; generally the prosecution may not introduce such evidence.

Rules of Evidence

An accused person is protected by rules of evidence concerned with the proof of facts. These are rigorously applied in British criminal trials. If evidence is improperly admitted, a conviction can be quashed on appeal.

The rules exclude evidence of a person's character or previous convictions except where it is relevant to the charges against the defendant. Hearsay evidence is generally inadmissible.

Appeals

A convicted person can appeal to a higher court against conviction or against the sentence passed, although leave to do so is sometimes required. An independent Criminal Cases Review Commission is being established to examine possible miscarriages of justice and to decide whether to refer them to the courts. In non-jury trials for terrorist-type offences in Northern Ireland, there is an automatic right of appeal without having to seek leave to do so; an appeal is decided by a panel of three judges.

Sentencing

In Britain no one can be imprisoned except for acts definitely forbidden by law at the time of their commission.

With the exception of the penalty for murder (mandatory life imprisonment), the penalty laid down by statute for a criminal offence is the maximum that can be imposed for the offence; within that maximum, the courts decide the sentence.

If legislation is passed to increase maximum penalties, the new maxima cannot be imposed for offences committed before the date on which the new powers come into effect. Lower maxima or new forms of sentence can, however, apply forthwith.

New legislation provides for sentence discounts for those pleading guilty at an early stage in the court process, giving effect to a recommendation of the Royal Commission on Criminal Justice.

Right to Privacy

Article 12. No one shall be subjected to arbitrary interference with his privacy, family, home or correspondence, nor to attacks upon his honour and reputation. Everyone has the right to the protection of the law against such interference or attacks.

Privacy and the Law

Liberty for the individual in his or her private life is secured by the law of the land, enforced by the courts. The common law allows people to speak and act in their own homes as they please and to carry on their daily business, provided that they do not infringe the rights of others or commit an offence.

Parents are able to bring up their children as they wish provided that they do not break laws against cruelty and exposure to moral and physical danger. Parents also have to observe the law on compulsory education of their children.

While it is a criminal offence for a man to commit a homosexual act with a person under the age of 18, homosexual acts in private by consenting men aged 18 or over are permissible.

Press Complaints Commission

In response to widespread concern about press standards, media intrusion into the privacy of individuals and inaccurate and biased reporting, the Press Complaints Commission, a non-statutory body, was set up by the newspaper and periodicals industry in 1991 in an attempt to make self-regulation of the press work properly.

The Commission, whose members are drawn from newspaper and magazine editors as well as people from outside the industry, deals with complaints by members of the public about the contents and conduct of the press, and advises editors and journalists. The Commission operates a code of practice agreed by editors governing respect for privacy, opportunity to reply, corrections, journalists' behaviour, references to race and religion and other issues. The industry and the Press Complaints Commission have reinforced voluntary regulation through:

—increasing the lay members to a majority of the commission;

—a strengthening of the code of practice;

—the setting up of a helpline service for members of the public; and

—the appointment of a Privacy Commissioner with special powers to investigate complaints about privacy.

In its White Paper, *Privacy and Media Intrusion*, published in July 1995, the Government rejected proposals for statutory regulation of the press, and for legislation to give protection to privacy. Instead it endorsed self-regulation under the Commission and recommended further measures to make self-regulation more effective.

Other Intrusion

Some other forms of intrusion are criminal offences, for example, the use of unlicensed radio transmitters for bugging, the harassment of tenants to make them quit or the sending of unsolicited obscene material through the post. Other attempts to obtain private information may involve offences of criminal trespass. In some instances of intrusion on privacy, the civil law on trespass, contract and copyright or breach of confidence may provide a right of action leading to financial damages.

The law against libel gives protection against attack on a person's honour and reputation.

The right to privacy of some convicted offenders is safeguarded by legislation. Under this a person convicted of a criminal offence need not in general admit or reveal it after a rehabilitation period of from six months to ten years, depending on the nature or length of the original sentence. This law does not apply to people who have received prison sentences of more than two and a half years.

Interception of Communications

The Government may authorise the interception of postal and telephone communications but only on certain limited grounds. These are national security, the prevention or detection of serious crime, and the safeguarding of Britain's economic well-being. Unauthorised interception of communications is a criminal offence. An independent Commissioner (a senior judge) reviews the way in which interceptions are authorised and reports to the Prime Minister annually. Anyone who believes that his or her communications have been intercepted may apply to a Tribunal for an investigation; if the Tribunal concludes that an interception has been authorised in contravention of the law, it may quash the warrant, order intercepted material to be destroyed and award compensation.

Computers and Privacy

Legislation passed in 1984 gives protection against the threat to privacy posed by the use of computers to process personal information.

Under the Data Protection Act 1984, which gives effect to a Council of Europe convention, data users are required to register a description of the personal data they hold, the purposes for which they use it, the sources from which they obtain it and the categories of person to whom they may disclose it. They must also provide an address to which data subjects may write for access to the data.

Data users must comply with a number of principles. These state that the information should be:

—collected and processed fairly and lawfully;

—held only for specified, lawful registered purposes;

—adequate and relevant and not excessive;

—accurate;

—kept up-to-date;

—kept no longer than is necessary;

—available to data subjects on request and, where appropriate, corrected or erased; and

—properly protected against unauthorised access, alteration, loss, disclosure or destruction.

Individuals have the legal right to know about the data held on them and the right to ask a court to have factually wrong or misleading data corrected or deleted. In addition, they have the right to claim compensation for damages if the data are lost, inaccurate or disclosed without authority.

The legislation is implemented by the Office of the Data Protection Registrar, which compiles, maintains and makes publicly available the register of data users and computer bureaux. It also ensures that these meet their obligations under the Act. The Registrar has power to serve notices enforcing compliance with the data protection principles and may de-register the data user or prosecute for non-compliance.

Some categories of personal data, such as that relating to national security, are exempt from the registration provisions. Data subjects may be denied access to personal data: for example, that held for law enforcement or revenue purposes which would be prejudiced if disclosure was made. Regulations limit data subjects' access to data held on physical or mental health or in connection with social work.

Freedom of Movement

Article 13. (i) Everyone has the right to freedom of movement and residence within the borders of each State.

(ii) Everyone has the right to leave any country, including his own, and to return to his country.

Citizens are free to go anywhere unless they are under some form of lawful detention or restriction arising from civil or criminal proceedings or subject to an exclusion order under prevention of terrorism legislation (see p. 19).

The police in England and Wales have power to stop and search people suspected of possessing stolen goods, offensive weapons or implements that could be used for theft, burglary or other offences. An officer must, however, state and record the reasons for taking this action and what, if anything, was found. These powers must be used sparingly and a code of practice approved by Parliament governs their use.

Police officers may stop and search all people and vehicles for offensive weapons and knives if violence is likely to break out. This power is linked to a specified time and area, and would require the authority of a superintendent or higher rank.

There is free choice of residence provided that the choice does not infringe the property rights or amenities of another person.

As with other states, any person entering Britain is required to produce a passport or other acceptable travel document satisfactorily establishing identity and nationality. A British passport in Britain is issued by the Passport Agency; in other countries this is done by the Foreign and Commonwealth Secretary through British diplomatic posts. Although a British citizen does not have a legal right to a passport, the power to withhold or withdraw such a document is exercised only in the most exceptional circumstances.

Political Asylum

Article 14. (i) Everyone has the right to seek and to enjoy in other countries asylum from persecution.

(ii) **This right may not be invoked in the case of prosecutions genuinely arising from non-political crimes or from acts contrary to the purposes and principles of the United Nations.**

Britain is a signatory of the 1951 UN Convention Relating to the Status of Refugees and its 1967 Protocol and continues to meet its obligations to refugees under these instruments.

The Convention defines a refugee as a person who has 'a well founded fear of being persecuted for reasons of race, religion, nationality, membership of a particular social group or political opinion'. Britain has traditionally granted asylum to individuals fleeing persecution. However, in the last few years there has been a significant change in both the numbers and the motivation of those seeking asylum in Britain.

The majority of asylum-seekers in recent years have not qualified for recognition as refugees. Many applicants do not arrive direct from the country in which they claim to fear persecution while others, not fearing persecution, have left poor or troubled areas in search of better prospects elsewhere. Many asylum-seekers are, therefore, motivated by economic factors.

This change is not limited to Britain. Throughout Europe the numbers seeking asylum have doubled every three years since the mid-1980s. The weight of numbers has overburdened the asylum procedures in receiving states. In Britain in 1995 over 64,400 applications were awaiting initial decisions.

In common with other European countries Britain reviewed its procedures in order to curb misuse of the system while safeguarding the interests of genuine refugees. The Asylum and Immigration Appeals Act 1993 provides for a more streamlined system to reduce delays while ensuring that asylum applicants have every opportunity to present their case and have negative decisions reviewed by independent adjudicators.

Britain and the other 14 members of the European Union have signed the Dublin Convention, which defines when a member state is responsible for dealing with an asylum application.

In addition to accepting refugees, Britain also grants exceptional leave to remain to a number of people who do not qualify under the Convention. This is done in circumstances when it would be unreasonable to return them to their own country. Britain is working with other countries, through the United Nations and other international fora, to identify durable solutions to the problems which give rise to refugee flows.

Britain's United Nations obligations are also reflected in its policy towards extradition requests from other countries. Under recent legislation people are not extradited to face trial or impris-onment if they face persecution on grounds of race, religion, nationality or political opinion.

British extradition law prevents extradition for political offences. But, in common with other Council of Europe member states, Britain is a signatory of the European Convention on the Suppression of Terrorism, which it has ratified. The effect of this is to prevent use of the political offence exception in cases of crimes of violence. Fugitives sought for such crimes may, however, still claim the protection of the broader safeguard described above which prevents extradition where they would be persecuted or prejudiced in the requesting state. The fugitive has a statutory right to see the papers on which the extradition request is based and can make a representation to the Home Secretary or the Secretary of State for Scotland if a committal order is made by a court. If the

Home Secretary or the Secretary of State for Scotland decides to return the fugitive, the latter can seek a judicial review of this decision. Return is delayed until the judgment is given.

Nationality

Article 15. (i) Everyone has the right to a nationality.

(ii) No one shall be arbitrarily deprived of his nationality nor denied the right to change his nationality.

Under the 1981 British Nationality Act there are three main forms of citizenship:

—British citizenship for people closely connected with Britain;

—British Dependent Territories citizenship for people connected with the dependent territories; and

—British overseas citizenship for those citizens of the United Kingdom and Colonies who did not acquire either of the other citizenships when the 1981 Act came into force.

British citizenship is acquired automatically at birth by a child born in Britain if his or her mother or father is a British citizen or is settled in Britain. A child adopted in Britain by a British citizen is a British citizen. A child born abroad to a British citizen born, adopted, naturalised or registered in Britain is generally a British citizen by descent. The Act safeguards the citizenship of a child born abroad to a British citizen in Crown Service, certain related services, or in service under a European Union institution.

British citizenship may also be acquired:

—by registration for certain children, including those born in Britain who do not automatically acquire such citizenship at birth, or who have been born abroad to a parent who is a citizen by descent;

—by registration for British Dependent Territories citizens, British Overseas citizens, British subjects under the Act, British Nationals (Overseas) and British protected persons after five years' residence in Britain, except for people from Gibraltar, who may be registered without residence;

—by registration for stateless people and those who have previously renounced British nationality; and

—by naturalisation for all other adults aged 18 or over.

British citizenship can be renounced by a person if he or she possesses, or is about to acquire, the nationality or citizenship of another country. A woman who is a British citizen does not lose her citizenship if she marries a non-British citizen. She may renounce it if she has another citizenship or nationality. The wife or husband of a British citizen may apply for naturalisation after spending three years in Britain instead of the normal five. These residence requirements may in certain circumstances be waived if an applicant is married to a British citizen who is in Crown or designated service under the British Government.

A person cannot be deprived of British citizenship against his or her will unless he or she was registered or naturalised as a result of fraud, misrepresentation or concealment of a material fact. A registered or naturalised citizen can be deprived of British citizenship on some other very exceptional grounds such as disloyalty. If it is intended to deprive a person of his or her British nationality, he or she has a right to be heard by a committee of inquiry; the Home Secretary must also be satisfied that the deprivation would be in the public interest.

Legislation passed in 1983 conferred British citizenship on Falkland Islanders who did not acquire it under the 1981 Act. Special arrangements covering the status of British Dependent Territories citizens connected with Hong Kong when the territory returns to the People's Republic of China in 1997 are made by the Hong Kong (British Nationality) Order 1986. Under this, such citizens are entitled, before 1997, to acquire a status known as British National (Overseas) and to hold a passport in that status. In addition, the British Nationality (Hong Kong) Act 1990 made provision for the registration as British citizens before 30 June 1997 of up to 50,000 people who are able to meet certain criteria, and who are recommended by the Governor, together with their spouses and children who are still minors.

Marriage and the Family

Article 16. (i) Men and women of full age, without any limitation due to race, nationality or religion, have the right to marry and to found a family. They are entitled to equal rights as to marriage, during marriage and at its dissolution.

(ii) Marriage shall be entered into only with the free and full consent of the intending spouses.

(iii) The family is the natural and fundamental group unit of society and is entitled to protection by society and the State.

Marriage

A man and a woman may marry provided that both are at least 18 years of age, that they are not closely related members of the same family and that neither of them is already married. Young people between the ages of 16 and 18 can marry on the same conditions; in England and Wales, however, they must have the consent of their parents, legal guardian or some authorised person, or, in the final instance, a court of law; the absence of such consent does not make the marriage void. Parental consent is not required in Scotland.

The law permits members of any religion to marry by means of a religious ceremony, provided certain formalities are conformed with. A marriage may also be authorised by a civil ceremony. All marriages are registered by the State.

It is unlawful to force anyone to marry against his or her will or to bring about a marriage by fraudulent means.

The Family

The law contains provisions to strengthen marriage and family ties and to maintain the integrity of the family as a social unit. Communications between wife and husband are, in English and Scots law, absolutely privileged against disclosure; this means that neither spouse can be compelled to disclose them in a court of law and they cannot be the subject of libel or defamation proceedings.

The sole ground for divorce throughout Britain is the irretrievable breakdown of marriage; there are provisions for ensuring that the arrangements for the children are satisfactory and for the maintenance of family members and the fair sharing of the family's property.

The Child Support Agency, and its counterpart in Northern Ireland, is responsible for assessing, collecting and enforcing child maintenance payments and for tracing absent parents.

Children

Children and young people cannot be removed from home without the consent of the parents, unless a court order or, in Scotland, a children's hearing order is made. Such orders can be made if children are deprived of a normal home life (for instance, through desertion by parents) or if they have to be removed from home for their own protection. If children are removed from home, local government social services authorities are required to care for them, help to bring families together and see how children can be safely reunited with their parents (see p. 76).

It is against the law to abduct a child to or from Britain. A parent who has right of custody of a child under the age of 16 can enforce these rights in countries party to the Hague Convention on the Civil Aspects of International Child Abduction and the European Convention on the Recognition and Enforcement of Decisions Concerning Custody of Children and on Restoration of Custody of Children. In such countries, the judicial or administrative authorities are required to consider an application for the return of a child without the parents having to fight a custody case in another country. They are not, however, bound to order the return of the child. Parents of children who have been abducted are eligible for legal aid.

Succession Rights

Members of the family are in an advantageous position in matters of succession. If death occurs without a valid will, the spouse and children of the deceased have priority. Children have equal rights of inheritance from parents whether the parents are married or unmarried.

If a will fails to make provision for a surviving wife, husband or any children, the law in Scotland enables a spouse or child to claim automatically a proportion of the estate. In England and Wales the court has power to make such provision.

Property

Article 17. (i) Everyone has the right to own property alone as well as in association with others.

(ii) No one shall be arbitrarily deprived of his property.

Every person in Britain has the right to use and dispose of his or her own property, subject only to the overriding interest of the community as a whole. Appropriation by the State is possible only with the authority of legislation approved by Parliament. This may take the form of taxation to meet the expenses of government, or compulsory purchase for such purposes as housing, road building, defence, distribution of industry or the redevelopment of decayed and inner city areas. Compensation is paid for any losses suffered through compulsory purchase or the deterioration of property as a result of activities by public authorities.

Theft, robbery, deception, blackmail, handling stolen goods or forgery are criminal offences. So is deliberate, serious or reckless damage to someone else's property. The criminal courts have power to make a compensation order against a convicted defendant; this takes precedence over a fine. Alternatively the victim may recover compensation for loss or damage in civil legal proceedings.

Religious Toleration

Article 18. Everyone has the right to freedom of thought, conscience and religion; this right includes freedom to

change his religion or belief, and freedom, either alone or in community with others and in public or private, to manifest his religion or belief in teaching, practice, worship and observance.

Worship and religious teaching in Britain[8] take place without any interference from the community or the State. There is complete freedom of thought, conscience and form of worship and no restriction on the right of any citizen to change his or her religion. Atheists, agnostics and humanists are also free to promote their views.

A person may, however, be held guilty of blasphemous libel if he or she publishes scurrilous and offensive references to Christianity that go beyond the limits of proper controversy. This does not apply to debate and discussion about the truth of Christian doctrines.

Most of the world's religious are represented in Britain. There are large Hindu, Jewish, Muslim and Sikh communities and also smaller communities of Baha'is, Jains and Zoroastrians, but Britain is predominantly Christian.

The past 30 years have seen an increasingly diverse pattern of religious belief and affiliation in Britain. This has been linked both to patterns of immigration and to new religious directions among some of the indigenous population. Social structures have been gradually changing to accommodate this. For example, arrangements are made at many places of work to allow members of the various faiths to follow their religious observances. Muslims, Sikhs and Hindus all have mosques, temples or prayer centres throughout the country.

Religious organisations and groups of all kinds may own property, conduct ceremonies such as weddings and funerals, run

[8] For further information see *Religion* (Aspects of Britain: HMSO, 1992).

schools and promote their beliefs in speech and writing. In England, Scotland and Wales enquiries are not made about religion in population censuses or other official returns; in Northern Ireland censuses contain an optional question about religious beliefs.

There is no religious bar to the holding of public office except in the case of the Sovereign, who must by law be a Protestant.

The Church of England and the Church of Scotland are the established 'official' churches, that is, churches legally recognised as official churches of the State. Their members, however, do not obtain any advantages from being members of an established church rather than of any other church. There is no established church in Wales or Northern Ireland.

In institutions such as hospitals, the armed forces and prisons, provision is made for people professing different religious denominations and different creeds. Clergy of the Church of England, the Church of Scotland and the Church in Wales provide spiritual care and are paid a salary for this part of their work. Clergy belonging to other religious groups may be appointed as necessary.

Schools

All schools financed from public funds must provide religious education and a daily act of collective worship for all registered pupils. Religious education is required for all pupils as part of the national school curriculum (see p. 91); syllabuses must reflect Christianity while taking account of the other main religions practised in Britain. Parents have the right to withdraw their children from such classes and from collective worship. Some publicly maintained schools are provided by religious denominations and receive varying amounts of public finance, according to type. In Northern Ireland a core syllabus has to be approved by the four main churches and this must be taught in all grant-aided schools.

Television and Radio

Television and radio programmes are broadcast on religious topics; these include religious services as well as programmes in which adherents of the main religions and non-believers discuss their views. Religious advertisements may be broadcast on commercial radio and television, provided that they comply with the guidelines issued by the Independent Television Commission and the Radio Authority (see p. 55).

Freedom of Expression

Article 19. Everyone has the right to freedom of opinion and expression; this right includes freedom to hold opinions without interference and to seek, receive, and impart information and ideas through any media and regardless of frontiers.

Full rights of opinion and freedom of expression exist. There are some restrictions, including the official secrets legislation and laws concerning civil defamation, criminal libel, obscenity, sedition, incitement to racial hatred (see p. 19) and contempt of court.

It is a criminal offence to publish certain categories of official information whose disclosure might endanger national security or on other grounds. The courts decide whether harm is likely to arise as a result of such disclosure.

There are some restrictions on court reporting (see p. 33) to prevent any damage to the courts' reputation for fairness. If these are ignored, the publisher can be held to be in contempt of court. A fair and accurate report of legal proceedings is not regarded as contempt of court.

There are legal remedies against defamation. Fair comment on matters of public interest may be a defence. Proof that the alleged defamatory matter is true is also a defence. In the same way frank discussion of sexual problems is not considered to be an infringement of the law on obscenity.

The Press

There is no state control or censorship of the press, which caters for a range of political views, interests and levels of education. Newspapers are almost always financially independent of any political party. Where they express pronounced views and show obvious political leanings in their editorial comments, these derive from proprietorial and other non-party influences. A few newspapers and periodicals are governed by trustee-type arrangements designed to preserve their independence. Foreign language papers are freely imported.

Broadcasting

British broadcasting[9] has traditionally been based on the principle that it is a public service accountable to the people through Parliament. While retaining the essential public service element, it now embraces the principles of competition and choice. Three public bodies have the main responsibility for television and radio services, to which nearly everyone has access throughout Britain:

—the BBC (British Broadcasting Corporation) broadcasts television and radio programmes;

—the ITC (Independent Television Commission) licenses and regulates non-BBC television services, including cable and satellite services; and

—the Radio Authority licenses and regulates all non-BBC radio services, including cable and satellite.

The responsibilities of these public bodies are set out in legislation. The Secretary of State for National Heritage is respon-

[9] For further information see *Broadcasting* (Aspects of Britain: HMSO, 1993).

sible for broadcasting policy generally and can issue directions on a number of technical and other matters. The Government, however, is not responsible for programme content or broadcasters' day-to-day conduct of business.

Programme Standards

The independence of the broadcasters requires them to maintain certain standards regarding programmes and programme content. Under the relevant legislation and codes of practice operated by the broadcasting authorities, programmes must display, as far as possible, a proper balance and wide range of subject matter, impartiality in matters of controversy and accuracy in news coverage and must not offend against good taste. There are also rules relating to the portrayal of violence and to standards of taste and decency in television programmes, particularly during hours when large numbers of children are likely to be watching. Broadcasters must also comply with the general law relating to obscenity and incitement to racial hatred. Unacceptable foreign satellite services receivable in Britain can be proscribed by the Government.

The Broadcasting Standards Council has statutory powers to deal with complaints about violence and sex and about standards of taste and decency in television and radio programmes, and has a code of practice covering these issues. The broadcasters' own codes have to reflect the Council's code. Broadcasters can be required to publish the Council's findings on complaints.

The Broadcasting Complaints Commission, an independent statutory body, deals with complaints of unfair treatment in broadcast programmes and of unwarranted infringement of privacy in programmes. Details about adjudications are published by the broadcasters concerned.

The BBC has its own unit to investigate serious complaints about its programmes.

The Broadcasting Companies

The domestic services of the BBC are financed mainly from the sale of television licences. The BBC operates two national television networks, five national radio services, and regional services in Scotland, Wales and Northern Ireland. It also has 37 local radio stations.

The ITC regulates the commercial companies providing television services: ITV (Channel 3) and Channel 4. Both these channels are financed by advertising revenue. There are plans for a fifth television channel, also financed by advertising. The Radio Authority regulates all commercially financed local radio services and the three national commercial radio stations which have come on air since 1992.

Parliamentary and Political Broadcasting

Parliamentary debates and the proceedings of parliamentary committees of both Houses of Parliament are broadcast on television and radio, either live or more usually in recorded and edited form on news and current affairs programmes.

The BBC and the commercial services provide free time on radio and television for an annual series of party political broadcasts under rules agreed by the main political parties. Party election broadcasts are arranged following the announcement of a general election. In addition the Government may make ministerial broadcasts on radio and television, with opposition parties also being allotted broadcast time.

Cable and Satellite Channels

Licences to run British-based satellite television channels are granted, on a non-competitive basis, to programme services which are likely to meet consumer protection standards and are run by suitably qualified people.

BSkyB (British Sky Broadcasting) is the largest satellite programmer, providing nine channels. Other satellite channels available to British viewers include Eurosport, CNN (news), MTV (pop videos) and TV Asia. The choice available is expanding steadily. The ITC's various codes of practice apply to these programmes.

Franchises for providing cable services have already been granted covering areas which include two-thirds of all homes and nearly all urban areas in Britain. Regulation is as light as possible to encourage the development of a wide range of services, and flexible enough to adapt to new technology. Cable investment must be privately financed.

Britain has implemented two important European agreements on cross-border broadcasting. Under these, countries have to remove restrictions on the retransmission of programmes originating from other participating countries. They must also ensure that their own broadcasters observe certain minimum standards on advertising, sponsorship, taste and decency and the portrayal of sex and violence on television.

The Theatre

There is no censorship of plays. It is, however, a criminal offence to present or direct an obscene performance of a play in public or private. Such a performance is defined as one which, taken as a whole, tends to 'deprave and corrupt persons who are likely to attend it'. There is a defence against an obscenity charge on the grounds that the performance is for the public good in the interests of drama, opera or literature.

Films and Video

The Government does not have the power to censor films. Cinemas are licensed by local government authorities, which have a legal duty to prohibit the admission of children under 16 to unsuitable films. The licensing authority may also prevent the showing of any film, although this power is hardly ever exercised. In assessing the suitability of films, authorities normally rely on the judgment of the British Board of Film Classification, an independent non-statutory body to which films offered to the public must be submitted. The Board groups films into one of six categories, according to suitability for different age groups. The Board can require cuts to be made before a certificate is granted; it very rarely refuses a certificate.

The Board also has a certification system for videos, which is similar to that for films. It is an offence to supply commercially an unclassified video or to supply it to the wrong age groups.

Customs and Excise officials have power to seize any indecent article, including films or videos, imported into Britain.

Assemblies and Associations

Article 20. (i) Everyone has the right to freedom of peaceful assembly and association.

(ii) No one may be compelled to belong to an association.

People may assemble and demonstrate provided that they do so within the law. They may also organise and take part in processions. Organisers of processions must normally give the police notice of the event. The police may impose conditions on numbers, location and route if they believe that a demonstration or procession could result in serious public disorder, damage to property or serious disruption to the life of the community. Processions may be banned, with the Home Secretary's consent, only if serious public disorder cannot be avoided by the imposition of conditions. The wearing of political uniforms is prohibited.

Everyone has the right to join an association. An individual can be prosecuted if he or she agrees to do an unlawful act or a lawful act by unlawful means. A person can be sued for damages or an injunction if involved in a civil conspiracy; this is defined as a combination to cause damage to someone without lawful justification and which is carried into effect.

Associations organised to usurp the functions of the police or the armed forces are unlawful. The use of force for political ends is also against the law. The Government has powers to ban terrorist organisations (see p. 18).

Political Rights

Article 21. (i) Everyone has the right to take part in the government of his country, directly or through freely chosen representatives.

(ii) Everyone has the right of equal access to public service in his country.

(iii) The will of the people shall be the basis of the authority of government; this will shall be expressed in periodic and genuine elections which shall be by universal and equal suffrage and shall be held by secret vote or by equivalent free voting procedures.

Parliamentary Democracy

Britain is a parliamentary democracy,[10] the Government being responsible to the people through the elected House of Commons, which has the power to force a government to resign on a vote of no-confidence. Ministers are also accountable to Commons committees which monitor the work of government departments. The Commons consists of 651 Members of Parliament (MPs) directly elected by voters in each of Britain's 651 parliamentary constituencies.

The other House in Parliament is the non-elected House of Lords, which is normally a chamber of discussion and revision of proposals and not a rival to the Commons. It consists of hereditary and life peers. The Lords' powers to delay legislation are limited by law. It cannot delay legislation dealing only with taxation or expenditure. If the two Houses differ on non-financial Commons legislation, the Lords can delay it for no more than 13 months.

Elections to the Commons must take place within five years of the previous general election. If a Commons member resigns or dies during the life of a Parliament, a by-election is held.

Elected local councils are responsible for providing a wide range of public services. Councillors normally serve for a four-year term and elections are held at regular intervals. A by-election takes place if a councillor dies or resigns while in office.

British citizens, other Commonwealth citizens and citizens of the Irish Republic resident in Britain have the right to vote in parliamentary and local government elections if they are aged 18 years or over. Some people are not allowed to vote. These include:

[10] For further information see the following titles in the Aspects of Britain series: *The British System of Government* (HMSO, 1994), *Parliament* (HMSO, 1994), *Parliamentary Elections* (HMSO, 1995) and *Organisation of Political Parties* (HMSO, 1994).

—foreign nationals, other than citizens of the Irish Republic resident in Britain;

—sentenced prisoners;

—people detained under mental health legislation; and

—people convicted within the previous five years of corrupt or illegal practices.

Members of the House of Lords cannot vote in parliamentary elections but may do so in local elections.

Candidature for parliamentary elections is open to people aged 21 or over who are eligible to vote and who are not disqualified in any way. Those disqualified from standing as a candidate for election include:

—undischarged bankrupts;

—people sentenced to more than one year's imprisonment;

—clergy of the Church of England, Church of Scotland, Church of Ireland and Roman Catholic Church;

—members of the House of Lords; and

—judges, some civil servants, some local government officers and members of the regular armed services and the police service.

Also disqualified are some members of public corporations and government commissions as well as members of parliament or assemblies of countries outside the Commonwealth.

There are also some statutory disqualifications for local government elections.

Candidates normally belong to one of the main political parties, although smaller political parties or groups also put forward candidates, and individuals may stand without party support. Candidates do not have to be resident in the constituencies for which they stand.

The secret ballot is used in all British elections. The electoral system is the 'simple majority' or 'first past the post' system. The candidate with the largest number of votes is elected.

Northern Ireland

Northern Ireland[11] is represented by 17 members of the House of Commons. There are 26 district councils elected by proportional representation and responsible for certain local services.

From 1921 to 1972 Northern Ireland had its own Parliament with responsibilities for a wide range of local affairs. Following the upsurge in intercommunal violence in the late 1960s, Northern Ireland was subsequently placed under the direct rule of the British Parliament in 1972.

Over the past 25 years successive British governments have attempted to find the basis for returning greater power to Northern Ireland's locally elected representatives but agreement has proved elusive. The Anglo-Irish Agreement in 1985 gave new impetus to co-operation between Britain and Ireland on matters affecting Northern Ireland. From 1990 the Government has sought a widely acceptable and comprehensive political settlement encompassing all the relevant relationships: those within Northern Ireland, those within the island and those between the British and Irish governments, through the promotion of round table talks in 1991 and 1992 and by bilateral discussions with the main Northern Ireland political parties and also with the Irish Government.

In December 1993 the British and Irish governments signed the Joint Declaration, which made it clear that any settlement would be based on the fundamental principles of democracy and consent, and

[11] For further information see *Northern Ireland* (Aspects of Britain: HMSO, 1995).

could be reached only by agreement between parties which have established a commitment to *exclusively* peaceful methods. This was followed by both the IRA and Loyalist paramilitaries announcing ceasefires on 31 August and 13 October 1994 respectively.

Building on the Joint Declaration, the *Frameworks for the Future* document was launched in February 1995. This outlines what a comprehensive settlement might look like and is intended not to be imposed but to facilitate the resumption of multilateral dialogue including the Northern Ireland constitutional parties and the British and Irish governments. The Government has also given an undertaking to put the outcome of the talks to the electorate of Northern Ireland for approval in a referendum. The Government is continuing to work to create the right conditions for all-party talks, with the aim of achieving an overall settlement.

The European Parliament

Voters in Britain and the other 14 members of the European Union elect representatives to the European Parliament, which examines texts of Community legislation, proposes amendments and questions the European Commission, the body responsible for drafting this legislation. Members of the Parliament also put questions to the Council of the European Union responsible for taking Community decisions. Debates are held during plenary sessions about draft legislation and other matters of importance to the citizens of member states. The Parliament adopts the Community's annual budget in agreement with the Council of the European Union. The Commission can be removed from office as a whole by a two-thirds majority of all members of the Parliament in a vote of censure.

Members of the Parliament are elected every five years, the most recent election taking place in 1994.

The three members from Northern Ireland are elected by proportional representation under a system known as the single transferable vote.

Public Service

Officials working in central and local government have a long tradition of political impartiality. A change of minister therefore does not involve a change of departmental staff and civil service functions remain the same whichever political party is in office.

Public office is open to men and women, without distinction on grounds of sex, religion, race or colour. Staff are recruited to the Civil Service and its executive agencies through fair and open competition solely on the basis of merit.

Citizen's Charter

The aim of the Government's Citizen's Charter (launched in 1991) is to raise the standard of public services and make them more responsive to their users. The Charter is a ten-year programme which is intended to be at the heart of the Government's policy-making throughout the 1990s.

The Charter applies to all public services, at both national and local levels, and the privatised utilities. Most major public services have published their own charters. (By mid-1995, 40 had been issued.)

The Charter sets out a number of key principles which users of public services are entitled to expect:

Standards

Setting, monitoring and publishing explicit standards for the services that individual users can reasonably expect. Publication of actual performance against these standards.

Information and Openness

Full and accurate information should be readily available in plain language about how public services are run, their cost and performance, and who is in charge.

Choice and Consultation

There should be regular and systematic consultation with those who use services. Users' views about services, and their priorities for improving them, should be taken into account in final decisions about standards.

Courtesy and Helpfulness

Courteous and helpful service from public servants who will normally wear name badges. Services available equally to all who are entitled to them and run to suit their convenience.

Putting Things Right

If things go wrong, an apology, a full explanation and a swift and effective remedy should be given. Well publicised and easy-to-use complaints procedures with independent review wherever possible should be available.

Value for Money

Efficient and economical delivery of public services within the resources the nation can afford, and independent validation of performance against standards.

Implementing the Charter

A Cabinet minister, the Chancellor of the Duchy of Lancaster, is responsible for the Charter programme. The Prime Minister also receives advice on the Charter from a Panel drawn from business, consumer affairs and education. The Panel works with the Citizen's Charter Unit and officials in all the departments to implement and develop the Citizen's Charter programme. A number of projects are in progress to ensure that the Charter becomes an integral part of all public services and that members of the public are aware of the standards of service to which they are entitled.

Open Government
In line with Citizen's Charter principles, the Government has a general policy of increasing the openness and accountability of public administration. In April 1994 it introduced a code of practice on access to government information. This commits the Government to release certain information as a matter of course and also to respond to requests for other factual information which it holds. The code is policed by the Parliamentary Ombudsman (see p. 25). A similar code of practice covering the health service came into force in June 1995.

As part of the same openness, the Government is also to propose legislation to provide rights of access to health and safety information and personal records. These rights would add to a number of existing rights of access to information in specific areas such as environmental information.

Social Rights

Article 22. Everyone, as a member of society, has the right to social security and is entitled to the realisation, through national effort and international co-operation and in accordance with the organisation and resources of each State, of

the economic, social and cultural rights indispensable for his dignity and the free development of his personality.

There is a comprehensive system of social security, a publicly financed National Health Service and a publicly maintained education system.

Article 23. (i) Everyone has the right to work, to free choice of employment, to just and favourable conditions of work and to protection against unemployment.

(ii) Everyone, without any discrimination, has the right to equal pay for equal work.

(iii) Everyone who works has the right to just and favourable remuneration ensuring for himself and his family an existence worthy of human dignity, and supplemented, if necessary, by other means of social protection.

(iv) Everyone has the right to form and to join trade unions for the protection of his interests.

Help for Unemployed People

The Employment Service, an executive agency of the Department for Education and Employment, helps unemployed people to find work through its job placement and other services and pays benefits and allowances to those entitled to them. Its programmes include:

—Jobclubs where training and advice in job-hunting skills are given;

—Restart courses designed to rebuild self-confidence and motivation and plan a course of action leading to employment; and

—Community Action where people can do voluntary work in the community while they look for work.

In addition extra help is provided for clients with special needs, for instance long-term unemployed people, people with disabilities, homeless people, disadvantaged inner-city residents, people with literacy problems and ex-offenders.

The Jobseeker's Charter includes provisions governing the standard of service for people using the agency. Local offices have introduced a number of innovations under the Charter to meet the need of users, for example, electronic noticeboards and appointment control systems.

Training

The Government is committed to encouraging the public and private sectors to work together on training the labour force. The 81 Training and Enterprise Councils (22 Local Enterprise companies in Scotland) are employer-led partnerships bringing together people at local level. Their main aim is to develop a skilled and enterprising workforce necessary for sustained economic growth and prosperity. For 1995–96 the English programme for Training and Enterprise Councils is £1,100 million.

The Councils manage the Training for Work programme, which aims to give mainly long-term unemployed people the skills and experience they need to help them to get and keep jobs. It offers a personal training programme which meets individual and local labour market needs.

Another scheme managed by the Councils is Youth Training, which provides broad-based vocational education and quality training to give young people the modern skills and qualifications they require to get worthwhile jobs. Other schemes include:

—Youth Credits which offer young people who have left full-time education an entitlement to join the labour market to train to approved standards. Credits can be presented to an employer or training provider in exchange for training; and

—Modern Apprenticeships which are designed to increase the number of young people trained to technician, supervisory and equivalent levels. An accelerated version of this scheme provides high-level training for those aged 18 and 19.

The Councils are also, through the Investors in People initiative, encouraging employers to invest effectively in the skills needed for business success. This initiative is based on a rigorous national standard which helps companies to improve their performance by linking the training and development of all employees directly to the achievement of business objectives. In 1995–96 the Government has made more than £56 million available for Councils to help organisations work towards the standard.

A new framework of the vocational qualifications system has been established by the National Council for Vocational Qualifications (see p. 97), which covers 86 per cent of the workforce. It develops a system of nationally recognised qualifications based on standards of workplace competence set by employers.

Equal Pay and Opportunities
The legislation on equal opportunities and equal pay for men and women is described on pp. 13-14.

Pay and Working Conditions
In most industries the pay and conditions of workers are settled by national and/or plant bargaining between employers and trade unions. Under legislation, information needed for collective bargaining is disclosed to trade unions by employers, subject to certain safeguards. Where there is no collective bargaining, pay is usually determined by management at local level.

The Advisory, Conciliation and Arbitration Service conciliates in industrial disputes in the private and public sectors and provides arbitration on request. In addition, the Service gives advice on all aspects of industrial relations and employment policies to employers, managers, trade unions, employee representatives and individuals.

Health and Safety

Laws impose duties on employers to ensure the health, safety and welfare of their employees in factories, offices, mines, building sites and all other work activities. Employees have a duty to take care of their own safety and that of their fellow workers.

Under these laws arrangements should also be made to:

— protect the public from risks arising from work activities;

— control the keeping and use of explosives and highly flammable or other dangerous substances; and

— control exposure to virtually all substances hazardous to health such as chemicals, fumes, dust and micro-organisms.

The Health and Safety Commission, accountable to Parliament through the Secretary of State for the Environment, is responsible for issuing guidance and codes of practice. It also makes recommendations to the Government on changes in legislation. The Health and Safety Executive (HSE) carries out Commission policies and enforces the legislation. Government ministers are empowered to make regulations dealing with health and safety; where appropriate these are supplemented by the Commission's codes of practice. Britain also implements other health and safety regulations in legally binding directives from the European Union.

Employers, in consultation with their employees, are responsible for working out health and safety arrangements for their workplaces. Those with five or more employees must draw up a written health and safety policy and inform their employees about it. In workplaces where trade unions are recognised, the union may appoint its own safety representatives to put forward workers' views on health and safety matters.

Health and safety legislation is enforced by inspectors appointed by the HSE, or, for premises such as offices, shops, hotels and restaurants, by local government authorities working under guidance from the Health and Safety Commission.

Inspectors have the power to issue a notice which stops any process or activity likely to lead to serious personal injury or ill health. The notice sets out the remedial action that must be taken before work restarts. Inspectors may also order a fault to be remedied within a specified time. They have the power to prosecute any person failing to comply with these notices and/or relevant statutory provisions.

Trade Unions

People may join trade unions, which have members in virtually every occupation and nearly 9 million members in all. In addition to negotiating pay and other conditions with employers, they provide benefits such as educational facilities, financial services, legal advice and aid in work-related cases.

Dismissals for union membership or non-membership are automatically unfair. It is also unlawful for an employer to refuse to employ someone on the grounds of membership or non-membership of a trade union. Individuals who believe that they have been dismissed or refused employment on these grounds may complain to an industrial tribunal.

Trade union leaders have been made more accountable to their members by changes in the law. A trade union is, for instance, required to ensure that its members elect its general secretary, its president and every member of its governing body. Elections must be held at least once every five years and be carried out by secret postal ballot of the union's members. The election must be held under independent scrutiny. Similarly, ballots of union members must be held, and their consent obtained, before any industrial action can take place. All union members also have the right to a statutory remedy if unjustifiably disciplined by their union, for example, for not striking or for crossing a picket line.

A trade union may establish a separate political fund if it wishes to use its money for what the law defines as 'political objects'. The membership must approve such arrangements by a majority vote in a secret ballot, which is subject to independent scrutiny. Approval for a political fund has to be reconfirmed by further ballots at not less than ten-year intervals. All union members have the right to contract out of paying contributions to a political fund.

Article 24. Everyone has the right to rest and leisure, including reasonable limitation of working hours and periodic holidays with pay.

Hours of Work and Holidays
Hours of work and holidays with pay are determined by discussion between employers and employees. The basic working week in England, Scotland and Wales is about 34 to 40 hours for a five-day week. Actual hours worked are often more, especially for manual workers. Overtime is paid at higher rates.

In April 1995 average weekly hours worked, including paid and unpaid overtime, were 41.9 for men and 37.6 for women.

Collective agreements usually provide for at least four weeks' paid holiday a year, with many employees having five weeks or more, including extra holidays based upon length of service. There are also seven or eight public holidays a year.

Article 25. (i) Everyone has the right to a standard of living adequate for the health and well-being of himself and of his family, including food, clothing, housing and medical care and necessary social services, and the right to security in the event of unemployment, sickness, disability, widowhood, old age or other lack of livelihood in circumstances beyond his control.

(ii) Motherhood and childhood are entitled to special care and assistance. All children, whether born in or out of wedlock, shall enjoy the same social protection.

Health

The National Health Service (NHS) provides comprehensive medical care which is available to all residents, regardless of their income.[12] The NHS is financed mainly out of general taxation. Some forms of treatment, such as hospital care, are provided free of charge; others are charged for.

People are free to choose their family doctor, dentist, optician and pharmacist, who have contracts with the NHS.

Under the Citizen's Charter initiative (see p. 64), the NHS is required to publish national and local charters setting out the rights of patients and the standards of care they can expect to receive.

Family Doctors

Family doctors provide the first diagnosis of an illness, give advice and may prescribe a suitable course of treatment or refer a patient

---

[12] For more information see *Social Welfare* (Aspects of Britain: HMSO, 1995).

for more specialised treatment elsewhere. About four-fifths of family doctors work in partnerships or group practices.

A full-time family doctor must be available for at least 26 hours a week at times convenient for patients. Free health checks must be offered to all new patients and to anyone who has not attended for three years. Pensioners over 75 receive annual health checks, in their GP's surgery or in their own home, if they want them. Examinations by family doctors are free of charge.

To assist people to choose their family doctors, GPs must provide, on request, a copy of their practice leaflet, which sets out information on the services which the practice provides. Patients pay charges for prescriptions, although in practice almost 80 per cent are supplied free, since charges do not apply to people on low incomes, children, expectant mothers, pensioners and certain other groups.

Dental Services

Proportional charges are made for most types of NHS dental treatment, including examinations, although people on low incomes receive free treatment, as do pregnant women, mothers who have had a baby in the past year and anyone below the age of 18. Care includes preventive measures as well as restorative treatment. Dentists are encouraged to practise more preventive dentistry for children. All patients are entitled to a treatment plan setting out what is proposed by the dentist.

Eye Care

Ophthalmic medical practitioners and ophthalmic opticians are the only people allowed to test patients' sight. Entitlement to free NHS sight tests is restricted to people on low incomes, anyone below the age of 18, and those people with particular medical needs. The rest of the population have to pay for an eye test.

Spectacles are sold by registered ophthalmic and dispensing opticians. Unregistered retailers can also sell spectacles, but not to children who are under 16 or to people who are registered blind or partially sighted. Children, people on low incomes and those requiring certain complex lenses receive a voucher to put towards the cost of their spectacles.

Hospital Services

NHS hospital treatment is free of charge. Since 1990 hospitals and other health service units (for example, ambulance services and community health services) may apply to become independent of direct local health authority control and establish themselves as self-governing NHS trusts. These are run by boards of directors and are free to employ their own staff and set their own rates of pay, carry out research and provide facilities for medical education and other training. NHS trusts obtain their income mainly from NHS contracts to provide services to health authorities and to family doctors who choose, as fundholders, to become responsible for their own budgets. Trusts may also treat private patients.

Under the Citizen's Charter initiative, hospitals are expected to set out for patients the standards of service they offer. In addition, they have to organise improved appointment systems for outpatients and give maximum waiting times for hospital treatment within the NHS.

Private Medical Care

Patients are free to seek private medical treatment and doctors, dentists, opticians and pharmacists are able to practise privately. NHS hospital doctors, too, can practise privately, subject to certain rules. NHS patients are sometimes treated at public expense in private hospitals in order to reduce waiting lists. About 12 per cent of the population are covered by private medical insurance schemes.

Personal Social Services

Personal social services are provided by local government social services authorities and by independent private and voluntary organisations for families with special problems, children deprived of a normal home life, people with mental illness or learning disabilities, and elderly and disabled people and their carers.[13] Major services include skilled residential and day care, help for people confined to their homes and various forms of social work. Much of the care given to elderly and disabled people is provided by families and self-help groups.

New policies on community care were implemented between 1991 and 1993. These are intended to enable vulnerable groups in the community to live as independently as possible in their own homes for as long as they are able and wish to do so, and to give them a greater say in how they live and how the services they need should be provided.

Families and Children

Social services authorities provide help for families facing special problems. This help includes services for children in need or at risk of harm or neglect, and support for family carers who look after elderly and other family members. They also help single parents. In addition, there is short-term accommodation for women, often with young children, whose home conditions have become intolerable.

---

[13] See *Social Welfare* (Aspects of Britain: HMSO, 1995).

The Children Act 1989, which came into force in England and Wales in 1991, rests on the belief that children are best looked after by their parents without resort to legal proceedings. The Act introduced the concept of 'parental responsibility', which means that both parents continue to play a part in the child's upbringing even if they are separated or divorced. Unmarried fathers have the right to share parental responsibility in agreement with the mother without having to go to court.

Under the Act local authorities have a duty to provide services to support families with children in need. Services must be provided in consultation and partnership with families; in addition, other statutory authorities and voluntary organisations are involved.

Day nurseries, playgroups and childminders for children under five are also provided by local authorities, voluntary agencies and privately. In 1993 the Government launched a £45 million childcare scheme for children over five after school hours and during the holidays. The scheme is operated through Training and Enterprise Councils and Local Enterprise Companies (see p. 68).

Many different agencies and professions are concerned with recognition, prevention and management of child abuse. Local area child protection committees discuss and draw up policies and procedures for handling these cases. There is training for health visitors, school nurses and local authority social services staff.

Under the Children Act a court can issue a short-term emergency protection order to prevent a child suffering significant harm; the order is made only if there is sufficient evidence.

Children in Care

Local government authorities must provide accommodation for children who have no parent or guardian, have been abandoned, or whose parents are unable to provide for them. Parents of children in care retain their parental responsibilities but act as far as possible as partners with the authority. Under the Children Act, the authority is required to prepare a child for leaving care and to continue advising him or her up to the age of 21. Local authorities are also required to have a complaints procedure with an independent element to cover children in their care. Recent official inquiries into the standards of council care have led to recommendations which are being implemented.

In England and Wales a child may be brought before a family proceedings court if he or she is neglected or ill-treated, exposed to moral danger, beyond the control of parents or not attending school.

The court can commit the child to the care of a local authority under a care order, which can be made only if the court is satisfied that the child is suffering or is likely to suffer significant harm because of a lack of reasonable parental care or is beyond parental control. However, an order is made only if the court is also satisfied that this will positively contribute to the child's well-being and be in his or her best interests. In court proceedings the child is entitled to separate legal representation and to have a guardian to protect his or her interests.

All courts have to treat the welfare of the child as the paramount consideration when reaching any decision about his or her upbringing. The family proceedings court consists of specially trained magistrates with power to hear care cases as well as all other family and children's cases.

In England and Wales criminal proceedings cannot be brought against children below the age of 10 years. Offenders between the ages of 10 and 18 fall within the jurisdiction of youth courts. Under a supervision order—which may remain in force for not more than three years—a child (10–13 years) or young person (14–17) normally lives at home under the supervision of a social worker or probation officer.

In Scotland children who have committed offences or are in need of care and protection may be brought before a children's hearing, which can impose a supervision requirement on a child if it thinks that compulsory measures are appropriate. Under these requirements most children are allowed to remain at home under the supervision of a social worker, but some may live with foster parents or in a residential establishment while under supervision. Supervision requirements are reviewed at least once a year until ended by a children's hearing. The Children (Scotland) Act 1995, which will come into force in 1996–97, implements proposals on Scottish child care policy and law published in 1993. In addition to the major legislative changes, a number of improvements in child care services, policy and practice have already been made.

In Northern Ireland the juvenile court may place children who are in need of care, protection or control into the care of a fit person (including a health and social services board or trust), or make them subject to a supervision order. Children in trouble may be required to attend an attendance centre, be committed to a training school, or be detained in a remand home. The Children (Northern Ireland) Order 1995 provides Northern Ireland with legislation broadly equivalent to the Children Act 1989 in England and Wales and creates a separation between the treatment of children in need of care and young offenders. The legislation is expected to come into force in October 1996.

Adoption

Local authorities are required by law to provide an adoption service, either directly or by arrangement with a voluntary organisation. Adoption is strictly regulated by law and voluntary adoption societies must be approved by the Government. The Registrars-General keep confidential registers of adopted children. Adopted people may be given details of their original birth record on reaching the age of 18, and counselling is provided. An Adoption Contact Register enables adopted adults and their birth parents to make contact if that is the wish of both parties. A person's details are entered only if they wish to be contacted.

A government White Paper on adoption in England and Wales, published in 1993, includes proposals to allow children aged 12 or over to agree to the making of their adoption order and to have the right to take part in their own adoption proceedings. In Scotland a review of adoption law published in 1993 led to a number of changes which were introduced in the Children (Scotland) Act 1995.

Social Security

The social security system[14] aims to provide financial help for people who are elderly, sick, disabled, unemployed, widowed, bringing up children or on very low incomes.

The system includes contributory national insurance benefits covering sickness, incapacity, unemployment, widowhood and retirement. There is also statutory sick pay and maternity pay paid for their employees by employers. Another part of the system consists of non-contributory benefits such as Child Benefit paid for every child in a family and a range of benefits for severely disabled people and those looking after them.

For people not in full-time work, whose resources are below certain levels specified by the Government, there is a non-contributory Income Support scheme designed to bring their income up to these levels. Family Credit is payable to low-paid employed and self-employed working families with children, where one parent works for at least 16 hours a week; it tops up their income without

[14] See *Social Welfare* (Aspects of Britain: HMSO, 1995).

destroying the incentive to increase their earnings. A similar scheme for disabled people in full-time work was introduced in 1992. A new benefit, Jobseeker's Allowance, will replace Unemployment Benefit and Income Support for unemployed people from October 1996.

There is also a housing benefit scheme and another to help pay council taxes; both are available to a broad band of low-income households and not only people receiving other income-related benefits.

Social security benefits are increased annually in line with percentage changes in retail prices.

A major programme to improve quality and customer service is in progress. The Benefits Agency, for example, is moving towards a easier system in which each customer's business with the Agency is handled by a single contact point.

Mothers and Children

Special preventive services are provided under the NHS to safeguard the health of pregnant women and mothers with young children. These include:

—free dental treatment for pregnant women;

—dried milk and vitamins for expectant mothers;

—vaccination and immunisation of children against certain infectious diseases; and

—health education before and after childbirth.

Since 1994 government policy has been to offer women more choice in maternity care provision and to move towards greater community-based care. Following comprehensive reviews of maternity care provision, the NHS is working towards implementing recommendations that the woman and her baby should be at the centre of all planning and provision in decisions on the care they receive.

Pregnant women receive ante-natal care from their family doctor and hospital clinics; women in paid employment have the right to visit the clinics during working hours. Nearly all women have their babies in hospital, returning home shortly after to be attended by a midwife or health visitor and, where necessary, the family doctor. Child-health centres and, increasingly, family doctors check the physical and mental health of pre-school children. Efforts have been made to improve co-operation between the community-based child health services and local authority social services on, in particular, the prevention of child abuse and the health and welfare of children in care.

There are voluntary programmes of immunisation against diphtheria, measles, mumps, rubella (women of child-bearing age and girls only), poliomyelitis, tetanus, tuberculosis and whooping cough. A new immunisation, 'Hib', was introduced in 1992, offering protection against invasive haemophilus disease, a major cause of meningitis in children under five years.

All pregnant employees have the right to 14 weeks' maternity leave. Any woman who has worked for the same employer for 26 weeks is entitled to Statutory Maternity Pay, with the first six weeks paid at 90 per cent of average weekly earnings, followed by a flat-rate payment for the rest of the leave.

If a woman does not qualify for maternity pay because, for example, she is self-employed, has recently changed jobs or given up her job she may qualify for a weekly maternity allowance. This is payable up to 18 weeks.

Britain is a party to the Council of Europe's convention on the legal status of children born to unmarried parents. This provides for common rules under which the legal status of such children is the same as for those born to a married couple. Legislation has been passed to remove former legal disadvantages suffered by children of unmarried parents.

Abortion
Under the Abortion Act 1967, as amended, a time limit of 24 weeks applies to the largest category of abortion—risk to the physical or mental health of the pregnant woman and also risk to any existing children of her family. There are three categories in which no time limit applies: to prevent grave permanent injury to the health of the woman; where there is a substantial risk of serious fetal handicap; or where continuing the pregnancy would involve a risk to the life of the pregnant woman greater than if the pregnancy were terminated.

An abortion must be performed by a registered medical practitioner and may be carried out only in an NHS hospital or in a place officially approved for the purpose.

The Act does not apply in Northern Ireland.

Human Fertilisation and Embryology
The birth of the world's first 'test tube baby' took place in Britain in 1978, using the technique of *in vitro* fertilisation. The social, ethical and legal implications were examined by a committee of inquiry in 1984 and led eventually to the Human Fertilisation and Embryology Act 1990, one of the most comprehensive pieces of legislation on assisted reproduction and embryo research in the world.

The Act set up the Human Fertilisation and Embryology Authority to license and control centres providing certain fertility treatments, undertaking human embryo research or storing gametes and embryos. The Authority maintains a code of practice giving guidance about licensed centres and reports annually to Parliament.

A child born by artificial insemination to a married woman is treated as a child of the woman's husband. In the case of an unmarried couple the man is regarded as the father and is required to maintain the child.

Surrogacy

Commercial surrogacy agencies and the advertising of, or for, surrogacy services are prohibited; legislation to ban the use of fetal ovarian tissue in fertility treatment was passed in 1994.

Housing

Between the end of 1971 and 1994 the proportion of owner-occupied housing[15] in Great Britain rose from nearly 50 per cent to 68 per cent in 1994. Most of the remainder is rented by public sector tenants or from private landlords.

Public Sector Housing

Local authority tenants in England and Wales have security of tenure and a number of other statutory rights, which are set out in the Council Tenant's Charter. These include:

— the right to buy their home at a discount (if they have been tenants for at least two years);

— the right to get certain urgent repairs done quickly and at no cost to them;

— the right to be paid for certain improvements they have made when they move home; and

[15] For more information see *Housing* (Aspects of Britain: HMSO, 1993).

—the right to take over the running of their estate through 'tenant management organisations'.

Over 90 such organisations have been set up and a further 100 are in development. Compulsory competitive tendering is being introduced for council house management to improve the quality of services. Tenants have to be closely involved in the process. Since 1979 over 1.6 million local council, housing association and new town properties have been sold in Great Britain under the right to buy. In addition since 1988 41 local authorities have transferred a total of almost 185,000 homes (with tenants' agreement) to housing associations under the Large Scale Voluntary Transfer scheme. Such transfers help to diversify the tenure of rented housing, and raise private funds to repair and improve the stock earlier than would have been possible had it remained with local authorities.

Housing Associations

Housing associations, which are non-profit-making, are the main providers of new low-cost housing for rent and for outright sale or shared ownership to those on low incomes. They own and manage over 750,000 homes and 65,000 hostel bed-spaces in England alone. Schemes are generally funded by a mixture of private finance and government grant. In 1995–96 about £1,200 million is being made available by the Government to housing associations. Tenants have the right to have the costs of repairs refunded if the association fails to carry out its obligations. A Tenants' Guarantee sets out benchmarks for assessing the quality of service on rents, maintenance and repair.

A Housing Association Tenants' Ombudsman Service was launched by the Government in 1993. The scheme, which covers England, allows independent investigation of tenants' complaints against their housing association; a similar scheme has been launched in Scotland, and one is being considered for Northern Ireland.

Housing Action Trusts

Housing Action Trusts are public bodies set up, following votes in favour by residents, to revitalise the worst housing estates over a period of 8–10 years. Trusts take over local authorities' housing and refurbish and redevelop it. They also aim to make long-lasting improvements to the economic, social and environmental conditions of their areas. Tenants are involved in all aspects of Trusts' work and elect representatives to their Boards. As Trusts complete their work, tenants can choose to return to local authority management, to transfer to a housing association or to form a tenant management organisation. There are six Trusts in England. Public expenditure on Trusts is £90 million a year.

Homeless People

Local government authorities have a statutory duty to ensure that accommodation is provided for people who are or about to become unintentionally homeless and who are in priority need—for example, pregnant women, people with dependent children or people who are vulnerable because of age, or physical or mental disability. Under the Government's six-year (1990–96) £182 million Rough Sleepers Initiative a range of accommodation has been provided to reduce the number of people sleeping rough in central London. It has funded the development of 3,300 places in houses and flats, 950 temporary hostel places, an annual winter shelter programme, and year-round outreach and resettlement workers. In addition since 1990 more than £20 million has been spent under the Homeless Mentally Ill Initiative to provide accommodation and psychiatric care for mentally ill people who have been sleeping rough in central London.

Grants totalling £6.9 million are being made available in 1995–96 to voluntary organisations to run projects which provide direct assistance to single people in need of accommodation. In Scotland extra money has been given to housing authorities for homelessness projects. Additional funding was announced by the Government in 1994 to tackle homelessness in Wales.

Privately Rented Housing

About 10 per cent of the housing stock in Britain is rented from private landlords. Government policy is to increase the availability of such accommodation through rent deregulation.

Two types of private tenancy were introduced in 1989 for new private sector letting.

—The assured tenancy gives long-term security of tenure in return for a freely negotiated market rent.

—The assured shorthold tenancy is for a fixed term, the rent being negotiated between landlord and tenant. Tenancies granted before 1989 where rents were fixed by an independent rent officer are unaffected by the change, although the rules relating to succession have been amended.

It is a criminal offence for a landlord to harass tenants. If tenants are driven out by harassment or illegally evicted, they must be compensated. If a landlord harasses or evicts a tenant in order to re-let at market rent, the courts may award damages to the tenant based on the profit made by the landlord. As a general principle, tenants and most other residential occupiers cannot be evicted without a court order.

Home Renovation Grants

Publicly financed house renovation grants help private owners and some tenants with the costs of essential repairs. A mandatory grant enables houses to be brought up to a newer and more effective fitness standard, with discretionary grant available for other works. Grants of up to 100 per cent may be available, subject to a test of the applicant's resources. In certain circumstances grants are available for disabled people and for the repair of houses in multiple occupation.

Education, Science and the Arts

Article 26. (i) Everyone has the right to education. Education shall be free, at least in the elementary and fundamental stages. Elementary education shall be compulsory. Technical and professional education shall be made generally available and higher education shall be equally accessible to all on the basis of merit.

(ii) Education shall be directed to the full development of the human personality and to the strengthening of respect for human rights and fundamental freedoms. It shall promote understanding, tolerance and friendship among all nations, racial or religious groups, and shall further the activities of the United Nations for the maintenance of peace.

(iii) Parents have a prior right to choose the kind of education that shall be given to their children.

The aim of the Government's education policy is to raise standards at all levels of ability, to increase parental choice and to make post-school education more widely accessible and more responsive to the needs of the economy.[16]

Schools

Parents are required by law to see that their children receive full-time education, at school or elsewhere, between the ages of 5 and 16 in England, Scotland and Wales and between 4 and 16 in Northern Ireland.

The state education system is free, but a small proportion of children attend private fee-paying schools. Most state schools are provided by local government authorities and in Northern Ireland by education and library boards. However, some state schools are grant-maintained and self-governed; these schools are now financed directly from central government not from local authorities. A grant-maintained status is allowed if a ballot of parents approves such a change. Under legislation passed in 1993, non-grant-maintained schools must consider each year whether or not to hold a ballot to alter their status.

Over half of three- and four-year-old children in Britain receive education in nursery schools or classes or in infants' classes in primary schools.

Well over 90 per cent of the state secondary school population in England, Wales and Scotland attend comprehensive schools, which take pupils without reference to ability and provide a wide range of education for all or most of the children in a district.

Rights of Parents

Parents have a statutory right to express a preference for a particular school for their children. Schools are obliged to publish general

[16] For further information see the following titles in the Aspects of Britain series: *Education* (HMSO, 1995), *Education After 16* (HMSO, 1995) and *Education Reforms in Schools* (HMSO, 1994).

information about themselves and their public examination results to help parents in making their choice. Local education authorities have to meet the parents' wishes unless the school is full or, if selective, the child does not meet required academic standards. There is a right of appeal if parents' wishes are not met. Some schools have agreed arrangements for preserving their character (for example, as a church school—see p. 52) which allow the school to refuse to admit a child.

see p. 52

All schools in England and Wales are required to admit pupils up to the limit of their available physical capacity if there is sufficient demand on behalf of eligible children by parents.

Each publicly maintained school in England and Wales has a governing body responsible for the main policies of the school, including the appointment and dismissal of staff. Most maintained schools must have equal numbers of parent representatives and local authority governors. Similar arrangements apply in Scotland.

All schools have to be inspected every four years by approved and independent inspectors, and summaries of these reports are given to parents.

In England and Wales state schools have to give parents annual reports on their child's progress including details about:

—the child's progress in all National Curriculum subjects studied;

—progress in all other subjects and activities;

—the child's general progress and attendance record;

—the results of National Curriculum assessments and of public examinations taken by the child; and

—comparative results of pupils of the same age in the school and nationally.

A generally similar reporting system exists in Northern Ireland. In Scotland schools are advised to give parents information about their child's achievements in class, comments by teachers, and steps to build on success or overcome difficulties.

School Curriculum

England and Wales: The National Curriculum in England consists of the core subjects of English, mathematics and science, and seven other foundation subjects: technology, history, geography, music, art, physical education and, for secondary pupils, a modern foreign language.

In addition, in Wales, Welsh is a core subject in Welsh-speaking schools and a foundation subject in non-Welsh-speaking schools. Nearly all primary schools in Wales teach Welsh as the sole or main medium of instruction. In secondary schools, Welsh is compulsory for pupils aged 11 to 16 in Welsh-speaking schools, and for pupils aged 11 to 14 in other schools. By August 1999 Welsh will be compulsory for almost all 11-to 16-year-old pupils.

For pupils aged 14 to 16, history, geography, art and music are all optional subjects, as are technology and a modern foreign language in Wales. In England the introduction of a modern language and technology as compulsory subjects has been postponed until September 1996.

Religious education is required for all pupils as part of the basic curriculum, and all secondary schools must provide sex education. Parents have a right to withdraw their children from these subjects.

Following a review in 1994, a revised National Curriculum was introduced for 5-to 14-year-olds in September 1995 and will be introduced for 14-to 16-year-olds from September 1996. The new streamlined requirements are designed to release more time for schools to use outside the statutory curriculum and give teachers more scope to use their professional discretion.

The National Curriculum now gives greater emphasis to information technology with the publication of separate programmes of study and attainment targets. Schools are also required to provide pupils with the opportunity to develop their information technology skills in all other National Curriculum subjects.

One of the Government's key objectives is to help young people develop the skills the economy needs. Education Business Partnerships, consisting of representatives from industry, education and the wider business community, aims to bring about closer links between education and industry in Great Britain and ensure that young people develop the skills to help them succeed in the labour market. One of the main schemes managed by the Partnerships is the Teacher Placement Service (which organises placements in business for teachers to improve learning opportunities for students and provide better career education services), while Compact networks have helped to increase the quantity and quality of these links by bringing together employers, young people, schools and colleges in order to help young people achieve more at school and to continue education and training after the age of 16. At present over 90 per cent of secondary schools in England have links with business, and nine out of ten pupils undertake work experience placements in their last year of compulsory schooling.

Northern Ireland: Pupils in Northern Ireland study the Northern Ireland Curriculum from the beginning of statutory schooling at the age of 4. The six broad areas of study are: English, mathematics, science and technology, the environment and society, creative and expressive studies and (for 11-to 14-year-olds only) language studies. There are also six compulsory cross-curricular themes—information technology, health education, education for mutual understanding, and cultural heritage—which must be studied from age 4 to 16, while economic awareness and careers education are compulsory for 11-to 14-year-olds. Schools must also provide religious education for all pupils, but sex education is not required as a separate subject.

As in England and Wales, the curriculum requirements were reviewed in 1994, leading to a slimmed-down compulsory curriculum in primary schools (ages 4 to 11 in Northern Ireland), and greater scope for schools to teach to the strengths of their 14-to 16-year-old pupils. These new arrangements will come into operation in September 1996.

Scotland: In Scotland curriculum content is not statutorily prescribed. Pupils aged 5 to 14 study a broad curriculum based on national guidelines which set out the aims of study, the ground to be covered and the way that pupils' learning should be assessed and reported. Pupils in this age group study five curriculum areas: language, mathematics, environmental studies, expressive arts and religious and moral education. Progress is measured against five levels: A to E. The key aims of the 5 to 14 curriculum are to achieve breadth, balance, coherence, continuity and progression for all pupils.

After age 14 pupils take courses which lead to an award at Standard Grade of the Scottish Certificate of Education. The examination enables all pupils, whatever their level of ability, to follow suitable courses and gain awards. Pupils may also take other certificated short courses provided by the Scottish Examination Board, and courses in a wide range of vocational courses offered by the Scottish Vocational Education Council. These vocational qualifications can be built up in the course of further education.

Celtic Languages
In addition to the arrangements for teaching Welsh in the curriculum in Wales (see p. 91), provision is made for teaching

Gaelic in Gaelic-speaking areas of Scotland, and in some other areas where education authorities have identified this as a priority. There are also a small number of grant-aided schools in Northern Ireland which teach through the medium of Irish.

Special Educational Needs

In the case of pupils with learning difficulties, local education authorities are required to:

—identify, assess and secure provision for the pupil's educational needs; and

—give parents the right to be involved in decisions about their children's education.

The initial assessment may lead to a Statement of Special Educational Needs being drawn up. This will set out the help the pupil requires and name the school which the pupil should attend. A code of practice has been issued offering guidance to local educational authorities and the governing bodies of all maintained schools in England and Wales on how to identify, assess and monitor all pupils with special educational needs. In Northern Ireland a code of practice will be issued in conjunction with new special educational needs legislation.

Wherever possible, pupils with special educational needs are educated in ordinary schools provided that the parents' wishes have been taken into account and that this is compatible with the provision of efficient education for the other pupils at the school. Otherwise, provision is made in special units or classes, or in day or residential special schools.

Ethnic Minorities

A substantial number of ethnic minority pupils have particular needs arising from cultural differences, including those of language, religion and custom. To meet these needs, English language teaching is given priority, together with a growing awareness of the value of bilingual support in the early primary years. Schools may teach the main ethnic minority community languages at secondary level in England and Wales as part of the National Curriculum. In setting their curriculum, schools should take account of, and reflect, the diversity of ethnic and cultural backgrounds of pupils at the school.

The Government has made it plain that racial discrimination has no place in the education service. A code of practice for the elimination of racial discrimination in education has been published by the Commission for Racial Equality. To ensure that education meets the needs of all pupils, the Government began in 1991 to collect annual statistics on the ethnic origins, languages and religions of pupils.

Post-school Education

In 1992–93 some 71 per cent of 16-year-olds took part in full-time further education, and an additional 16 per cent in part-time further education. This takes place in school sixth forms and further education colleges, including sixth form colleges. Also some 30 per cent of young people now enter universities and colleges of higher education.

Grants and Loans

The majority of those taking degree or equivalent courses are eligible for grants from public funds to pay for tuition fees and to help with living expenses; in addition, most home students on full-time higher education courses are eligible to apply for a student loan. Postgraduate students, except for those on a postgraduate course of initial teacher training, are not eligible to apply for student loans. Repayments, which are indexed in line with inflation, are due after completion of the course and can be deferred for a year at a time when income falls below 85 per cent of national average earnings.

Open University

Adults of all ages and backgrounds can study with the Open University. Entry to programmes is on a first-come first-served basis. No formal educational qualifications are required. Students typically study at home in their own time from a multi-media mix using specially written study units, television, video, audio cassettes and radio, work assignments and tutorials. There are also summer schools and local centres for contact with tutors and fellow students. Those studying for a BSc or a BA degree course typically begin with a foundation course and go on to study courses at higher levels later. Students are awarded a degree once they have built up the required number of course credits. This normally takes between three and six years. Students can also study with the Open University for higher degrees and professional development courses.

Further Education Colleges

People over the age of 16 can take courses in further education colleges. In April 1993 sixth form colleges were transferred from the schools sector, and joined existing further education colleges to form the new further education sector. Much further education is work-related and vocational. Some students on vocational courses attend part-time, either in the evenings or released by their employers, who are often involved in designing courses and are represented on college governing bodies. Students can also study for examinations which are the main standard for entry into higher education or professional training. Many courses lead to National Vocational Qualifications or Scottish Vocational Qualifications which have five levels of achievement, ranging from foundation to professional and mid-management. Students may also choose to take broader-based General National Vocational Qualifications.

Schools

Students can also stay on at sixth forms in schools, where most of the educational provision has been geared towards studying for examinations which are the main standard for entry into higher education or professional training. Many schools have also introduced vocational courses into their sixth form provision. Equality of status for academic and vocational qualifications is being promoted in England, Wales and Northern Ireland so that the new vocational qualifications now provide preparation for a range of occupations and higher education.

In Scotland pupils staying on at school study for higher grade examinations (Highers) which are the basis for entry into higher education or professional training. Vocational courses for 16- to 18-year-olds include business and administration, engineering and industrial production. Plans were announced in 1994 for new system of courses and awards that will involve a unified system of curriculum and assessment for Higher and vocational qualifications.

Article 27. (i) Everyone has the right freely to participate in the cultural life of the community, to enjoy the arts and to share in scientific advancement and its benefits.

(ii) Everyone has the right to the protection of the moral and material interests resulting from any scientific, literary or artistic production of which he is the author.

The Arts

Government policies aim to develop high standards of artistic and cultural activity, to encourage innovation, and promote public access to and appreciation of arts, crafts and the cultural heritage. The Government and local government authorities give financial support to the arts, while also encouraging partnership with the private sector, including business sponsorship.

In England responsibility for the Government's arts policy rests with the Secretary of State for National Heritage. The department administers government spending on national museums and galleries in England, the Arts Council of England, the British Library and other national arts and heritage bodies. The Secretaries of State for Wales, for Scotland and for Northern Ireland are responsible for arts in their countries, including the national museums, galleries and libraries, and the running of their respective arts councils. The preservation of the artistic heritage is encouraged by tax relief and other measures, including certain controls on the export of works of art.

The main channels for government aid to the performing arts are the independent Arts Councils of England, Scotland, Wales and Northern Ireland. These allocate funds to the major opera, dance and drama companies, symphony orchestras, small touring theatres, experimental groups and creative artists. This 'arm's length' approach in providing funds indirectly helps to avoid political influence over funding decisions by ensuring that funds are allocated by those best qualified to do so.

The government-funded British Film Institute encourages film, video and television as an art form.

Research on Science and Technology

The Government's strategy on science and technology[17] is to improve Britain's competitiveness and quality of life by maintaining the excellence of science, engineering and technology and by:

—developing stronger partnerships with and between science and engineering communities, industry and the research councils;

—supporting the science and engineering base in order to advance knowledge, increase understanding, and produce highly educated and trained scientists and technologists;

—contributing to international research;

—promoting the public understanding of science, technology and engineering; and

—ensuring government-funding research is conducted efficiently and effectively.

The Government considers that public funding should support the pursuit of basic scientific knowledge, with industry bearing the chief responsibility for the commercial development of scientific advances.

The Government's Office of Science and Technology, headed by the Chief Scientific Adviser, is responsible for seven research councils funded by the Government. These councils support research, study and training in universities and other higher education establishments, through their own institutes and

[17] For further information see *Science and Technology* (Aspects of Britain: HMSO, 1995).

international research centres. Government departments fund research and development related to their responsibilities.

Britain is also an active participant in European Union science and research programmes and in the EUREKA scheme, which encourages European co-operation in developing and producing high technology products with worldwide sales potential. Britain has concluded a number of inter-governmental and inter-agency agreements with other countries for co-operation in science and technology.

The British Council promotes better understanding and knowledge of Britain and its scientific and technological achievement. It encourages exchanges of specialists and fosters co-operation in research, training and education. It also manages technological, scientific and educational projects in developing countries.

Copyright and Patents

Original literary, dramatic, musical or artistic works, films, sound recordings and broadcasts are automatically protected by copyright in Britain. This protection is also given to works from countries party to international copyright conventions. The copyright owner has rights against unauthorised reproduction, public performance and broadcasting and issue to the public of his or her work; and against dealing in unauthorised copies. In most cases the author is the first owner of the copyright, its term being the life of the author and a period of 50 years after death (50 years from the year of release for films and sound recordings and 50 years from the year of broadcast for broadcasts).

Authors have the right to be identified on their works and to object to any derogatory treatment of them. Performers are also protected against making and trading in unauthorised recordings of live performance, the term of protection being 50 years from the year in which the performance is given. The term of protection was extended from 50 to 70 years in July 1995.

A copyright work first published in Britain has automatic copyright in all member countries of the Berne Copyright Convention and the Universal Copyright Convention.

The law secures the rights of the originators of inventions, new industrial designs and trade marks. Protection is also available under the European Patent Convention and the Patent Co-operation Treaty; benefits may be claimed in other countries under the International Convention for the Protection of Industrial Property.

The Government has taken steps to protect the ownership of ideas by means of patents, registered designs, trade marks and copyright. Measures include the adoption of EC directives on copyright which harmonise rental and lending rights, the rights of performers, record producers and broadcasters, and legal protection of computer programs; and a regulation on patents to create a supplementary protection certificate for medicinal products. The directive on computer programs has been implemented into law in Britain. Recent legislation has made provision for a new form of protection for designs and has made litigation regarding patents simpler and cheaper.

Safeguards for Human Rights

Article 28. Everyone is entitled to a social and international order in which the rights and freedoms set forth in this Declaration can be fully realised.

Article 29. (i) Everyone has duties to the community in which alone the free and full development of his personality is possible.

(ii) In the exercise of his rights and freedoms, everyone shall be subject only to such limitations as are determined by law solely for the purpose of securing due recognition and respect for the rights and freedoms of others and of meeting the just requirements of morality, public order and the general welfare in a democratic society.

(iii) These rights and freedoms may in no case be exercised contrary to the purposes and principles of the United Nations.

Article 30. Nothing in this Declaration may be interpreted as implying for any State, group or person, any right to engage in any activity or to perform any act aimed at the destruction of any of the rights and freedoms set forth herein.

As this book has shown, successive British governments have sought to strike a balance between the rights and freedoms of the individual and the general welfare of society as a whole. At the same time they have believed that the concentration of power in the hands of the executive as a means of curbing selfish interests for the sake of the public good must be strictly defined, for unless limitations are imposed, liberty can be imperilled.

Texts of International Human Rights Documents

INTERNATIONAL COVENANT ON ECONOMIC, SOCIAL AND CULTURAL RIGHTS

PREAMBLE

The States Parties to the present Covenant,

Considering that, in accordance with the principles proclaimed in the Charter of the United Nations recognition of the inherent dignity and of the equal and inalienable rights of all members of the human family is the foundation of freedom, justice and peace in the world,

Recognizing that these rights derive from the inherent dignity of the human person,

Recognizing that, in accordance with the Universal Declaration of Human Rights, the ideal of free human beings enjoying freedom from fear and want can only be achieved if conditions are created whereby everyone may enjoy his economic, social and cultural rights, as well as his civil and political rights,

Considering the obligation of States under the Charter of the United Nations to promote universal respect for, and observance of, human rights and freedoms,

Realizing that the individual, having duties to other individuals and to the community to which he belongs, is under a responsibility to strive for the promotion and observance of the rights recognized in the present Covenant,

Agree upon the following articles:

PART I
ARTICLE 1

1. All peoples have the right of self-determination. By virtue of that right they freely determine their political status and freely pursue their economic, social and cultural development.

2. All peoples may, for their own ends, freely dispose of their natural wealth and resources without prejudice to any obligations arising out of international economic co-operation, based upon the principle of mutual benefit, and international law. In no case may a people be deprived of its own means of subsistence.

3. The States Parties to the present Covenant, including those having responsibility for the administration of Non-Self-Governing and Trust Territories shall promote the realization of the right of self-determination, and shall respect that right, in conformity with the provisions of the Charter of the United Nations.

PART II
ARTICLE 2

1. Each State Party to the present Covenant undertakes to take steps, individually and through international assistance and co-operation, especially economic and technical, to the maximum of its available resources, with a view to achieving progressively the full realization of the rights recognized in the present Covenant by all appropriate means, including particularly the adoption of legislative measures.

2. The States Parties to the present Covenant undertake to guarantee that the rights enunciated in the present Covenant will be exercised without discrimination of any kind as to race, colour, sex, language, religion, political or other opinion, national or social origin, property, birth or other status.

3. Developing countries, with due regard to human rights and their national economy, may determine to what extent they would guarantee the economic rights recognized in the present Covenant to non-nationals.

ARTICLE 3

The States Parties to the present Covenant undertake to ensure the equal right of men and women to the enjoyment of all economic, social and cultural rights set forth in the present Covenant.

ARTICLE 4

The States Parties to the present Covenant recognize that, in the enjoyment of those rights provided by the State in conformity with the present Covenant, the State may subject such rights only to such limitations as are determined by law only in so far as this may be compatible with the nature of these rights and solely for the purpose of promoting the general welfare in a democratic society.

ARTICLE 5

1. Nothing in the present Covenant may be interpreted as implying for any State, group or person any right to engage in any activity or to perform any act aimed at the destruction of any of the rights or freedoms recognized herein, or at their limitation to a greater extent than is provided for in the present Covenant.

2. No restriction upon or derogation from any of the fundamental human rights recognized or existing in any country in virtue of law, conventions, regulations or custom shall be admitted on the pretext that the present Covenant does not recognize such rights or that it recognizes them to a lesser extent.

PART III
ARTICLE 6

1. The States Parties to the present Covenant recognize the right to work, which includes the right of everyone to the opportunity to gain his living by work which he freely chooses or accepts, and will take appropriate steps to safeguard this right.

2. The steps to be taken by a State Party to the present Covenant to achieve the full realization of this right shall include technical and vocational guidance and training programmes, policies and techniques to achieve steady economic, social

and cultural development and full and productive employment under conditions safeguarding fundamental political and economic freedoms to the individual.

ARTICLE 7

The States Parties to the present Covenant recognize the right of everyone to the enjoyment of just and favourable conditions of work, which ensure, in particular:

(*a*) Remuneration which provides all workers, as a minimum, with:

(i) Fair wages and equal remuneration for work of equal value without distinction of any kind, in particular women being guaranteed conditions of work not inferior to those enjoyed by men, with equal pay for work;

(ii) A decent living for themselves and their families in accordance with the provisions of the present Covenant;

(*b*) Safe and healthy working conditions;

(*c*) Equal opportunity for everyone to be promoted in his employment to an appropriate higher level, subject to no considerations other than those of seniority and competence;

(*d*) Rest, leisure and reasonable limitation of working hours and periodic holidays with pay, as well as remuneration for public holidays.

ARTICLE 8

1. The States Parties to the present Covenant undertake to ensure:

(*a*) The right of everyone to form trade unions and join the trade union of his choice, subject only to the rules of the organization concerned, for the promotion and protection of his economic and social interests. No restrictions may be placed on the exercise of this right other than those prescribed by law and which are necessary in a democratic society in the interests of national security or public order or for the protection of the rights and freedoms of others;

(*b*) The right of trade unions to establish national federations or confederations and the right of the latter to form or join international trade union organizations;

(*c*) The right of trade unions to function freely subject to no limitations other than those prescribed by law and which are necessary in a democratic society in the interests of national security or public order or for the protection of the rights and freedoms of others;

(*d*)   The right to strike, provided that it is exercised in conformity with the laws of the particular country.

2. This article shall not prevent the imposition of lawful restrictions on the exercise of these rights by members of the armed forces or of the police or of the administration of the State.

3. Nothing in this article shall authorize States Parties to the International Labour Organisation Convention of 1948 concerning Freedom of Association and Protection of the Right to Organize to take legislative measures which would prejudice, or apply the law in such a manner as would prejudice, the guarantees provided for in that Convention.

ARTICLE 9

The States Parties to the present Covenant recognize the right of everyone to social security, including social insurance.

ARTICLE 10

The States Parties to the present Covenant recognize that:

1. The widest possible protection and assistance should be accorded to the family, which is the natural and fundamental group unit of society, particularly for its establishment and while it is responsible for the care and education of dependent children. Marriage must be entered into with the free consent of the intending spouses.

2. Special protection should be accorded to mothers during a reasonable period before and after childbirth. During such period working mothers should be accorded paid leave or leave with adequate social security benefits.

3. Special measures of protection and assistance should be taken on behalf of all children and young persons without any discrimination for reasons of parentage or other conditions. Children and young persons should be protected from economic and social exploitation. Their employment in work harmful to their morals or health or dangerous to life or likely to hamper their normal development should be punishable by law. States should also set age limits below which the paid employment of child labour should be prohibited and punishable by law.

ARTICLE 11

1. The States Parties to the present Covenant recognize the right of everyone to an adequate standard of living for himself and his family, including adequate food, clothing and housing, and to the continuous improvement of living conditions. The States Parties will take appropriate steps to ensure the realization of this right, recognizing to this effect the essential importance of international co-operation based on free consent.

2. The States Parties to the present Covenant, recognizing the fundamental right of everyone to be free from hunger, shall take, individually and through international co-operation, the measures, including specific programmes, which are needed:

    (*a*) To improve methods of production, conservation and distribution of food by making full use of technical and scientific knowledge, by disseminating knowledge of the principles of nutrition and by developing or reforming agrarian systems in such a way as to achieve the most efficient development and utilization of natural resources;

    (*b*) Taking into account the problems of both food-importing and food-exporting countries, to ensure an equitable distribution of world food supplies in relation to need.

ARTICLE 12

1. The States Parties to the present Covenant recognize the right of everyone to the enjoyment of the highest attainable standard of physical and mental health.

2. The steps to be taken by the States Parties to the present Covenant to achieve the full realization of this right shall include those necessary for:

    (*a*) The provision for the reduction of the stillbirth rate and of infant mortality and for the healthy development of the child;

    (*b*) The improvement of all aspects of environmental and industrial hygiene;

    (*c*) The prevention, treatment and control of epidemic, endemic, occupational and other diseases;

    (*d*) The creation of conditions which would assure to all medical service and medical attention in the event of sickness.

ARTICLE 13

1. The States Parties to the present Covenant recognize the right of everyone to education. They agree that education shall be directed to the full development of the human personality and the sense of its dignity, and shall strengthen the respect for human rights and fundamental freedoms. They further agree that education shall enable all persons to participate effectively in a free society, promote understanding, tolerance and friendship among all nations and all racial, ethnic or religious groups, and further the activities of the United Nations for the maintenance of peace.

2. The States Parties to the present Covenant recognize that, with a view to achieving the full realization of this right:

(*a*) Primary education shall be compulsory and available free to all;

(*b*) Secondary education in its different forms, including technical and vocational secondary education, shall be made generally available and accessible to all by every appropriate means, and in particular by the progressive introduction of free education;

(*c*) Higher education shall be made equally accessible to all, on the basis of capacity, by every appropriate means, and in particular by the progressive introduction of free education;

(*d*) Fundamental education shall be encouraged or intensified as far as possible for those persons who have not received or completed the whole period of their primary education;

(*e*) The development of a system of schools at all levels shall be actively pursued, an adequate fellowship system shall be established, and the material conditions of teaching staff shall be continuously improved.

3. The States Parties to the present Covenant undertake to have respect for the liberty of parents and, when applicable, legal guardians, to choose for their children schools, other than those established by the public authorities, which conform to such minimum educational standards as may be laid down or approved by the State and to ensure the religious and moral education of their children in conformity with their own convictions.

4. No part of this article shall be construed so as to interfere with the liberty of individuals and bodies to establish and direct educational institutions, subject always to the observance of the principles set forth in paragraph 1 of

this article and to the requirement that the education given in such institutions shall conform to such minimum standards as may be laid down by the State.

ARTICLE 14

Each State Party to the present Covenant which, at the time of becoming a Party, has not been able to secure in its metropolitan territory or other territories under its jurisdiction compulsory primary education, free of charge, undertakes, within two years, to work out and adopt a detailed plan of action for the progressive implementation, within a reasonable number of years, to be fixed in the plan, of the principle of compulsory education free of charge for all.

ARTICLE 15

1. The States Parties to the present Covenant recognize the right of everyone:

(*a*) To take part in cultural life;

(*b*) To enjoy the benefits of scientific progress and its applications;

(*c*) To benefit from the protection of the moral and material interests resulting from any scientific, literary or artistic production of which he is the author.

2. The steps to be taken by the States Parties to the present Covenant to achieve the full realization of this right shall include those necessary for the conservation, the development and the diffusion of science and culture.

3. The States Parties to the present Covenant undertake to respect the freedom indispensable for scientific research and creative activity.

4. The States Parties to the present Covenant recognize the benefits to be derived from the encouragement and development of international contacts and co-operation in the scientific and cultural fields.

PART IV
ARTICLE 16

1. The States Parties to the present Covenant undertake to submit in conformity with this part of the Covenant reports on the measures which they

have adopted and the progress made in achieving the observance of the rights recognized herein.

2. (a) All reports shall be submitted to the Secretary-General of the United
Nations, who shall transmit copies to the Economic and Social
Council for consideration in accordance with the provisions of the
present Covenant.

(b) The Secretary-General of the United Nations shall also transmit to
the specialized agencies copies of the reports, or any relevant parts
therefrom, from States Parties to the present Covenant which are also
members of these specialized agencies in so far as these reports, or
parts therefrom, relate to any matters which fall within the responsibilities of the said agencies in accordance with their constitutional
instruments.

ARTICLE 17

1. The States Parties to the present Covenant shall furnish their reports in
stages, in accordance with a programme to be established by the Economic and
Social Council within one year of the entry into force of the present Covenant after
consultation with the States Parties and the specialized agencies concerned.

2. Reports may indicate factors and difficulties affecting the degree of fulfilment of obligations under the present Covenant.

3. Where relevant information has previously been furnished to the United
Nations or to any specialized agency by any State Party to the present Covenant,
it will not be necessary to reproduce that information, but a precise reference to
the information so furnished will suffice.

ARTICLE 18

Pursuant to its responsibilities under the Charter of the United Nations in the
field of human rights and fundamental freedoms, the Economic and Social
Council may make arrangements with the specialized agencies in respect of their
reporting to it on the progress made in achieving the observance of the provisions
of the present Covenant falling within the scope of their activities. These reports
may include particulars of decisions and recommendations on such implementation adopted by their competent organs.

ARTICLE 19

The Economic and Social Council may transmit to the Commission on Human Rights for study and general recommendation or as appropriate for information the reports concerning human rights submitted by States in accordance with articles 16 and 17, and those concerning human rights submitted by the specialized agencies in accordance with article 18.

ARTICLE 20

The States Parties, to the present Covenant and the specialized agencies concerned may submit comments to the Economic and Social Council on any general recommendation under article 19 or reference to such general recommendation in any report of the Commission on Human Rights or any documentation referred to therein.

ARTICLE 21

The Economic and Social Council may submit from time to time to the General Assembly reports with recommendations of a general nature and a summary of the information received from the States Parties to the present Covenant and the specialized agencies on the measures taken and the progress made in achieving general observance of the rights recognized in the present Covenant.

ARTICLE 22

The Economic and Social Council may bring to the attention of other organs of the United Nations, their subsidiary organs and specialized agencies concerned with furnishing technical assistance any matters arising out of the reports referred to in this part of the present Covenant which may assist such bodies in deciding, each within its field of competence, on the advisability of international measures likely to contribute to the effective progressive implementation of the present Covenant.

ARTICLE 23

The States Parties to the present Covenant agree that international action for the achievement of the rights recognized in the present Covenant includes such methods as the conclusion of conventions, the adoption of recommendations, the furnishing of technical assistance and the holding of regional meetings and technical meetings for the purpose of consultation and study organized in conjunction with the Governments concerned.

ARTICLE 24

Nothing in the present Covenant shall be interpreted as impairing the provisions of the Charter of the United Nations and of the constitutions of the specialized agencies which define the respective responsibilities of the various organs of the United Nations and of the specialized agencies in regard to the matters dealt with in the present Covenant.

ARTICLE 25

Nothing in the present Covenant shall be interpreted as impairing the inherent right of all peoples to enjoy and utilize fully and freely their natural wealth and resources.

PART V
ARTICLE 26

1. The present Covenant is open for signature by any State Member of the United Nations or member of any of its specialized agencies, by any State Party to the Statute of the International Court of Justice, and by any other State which has been invited by the General Assembly of the United Nations to become a party to the present Covenant.

2. The present Covenant is subject to ratification. Instruments of ratification shall be deposited with the Secretary-General of the United Nations.

3. The present Covenant shall be open to accession by any State referred to in paragraph 1 of this article.

4. Accession shall be effected by the deposit of an instrument of accession with the Secretary-General of the United Nations.

5. The Secretary-General of the United Nations shall inform all States which have signed the present Covenant or acceded to it of the deposit of each instrument of ratification or accession.

ARTICLE 27

1. The present Covenant shall enter into force three months after the date of the deposit with the Secretary-General of the United Nations of the thirty-fifth instrument of ratification or instrument of accession.

2. For each State ratifying the present Covenant or acceding to it after the deposit of the thirty-fifth instrument of ratification or instrument of accession, the present Covenant shall enter into force three months after the date of the deposit of its own instrument of ratification or instrument of accession.

ARTICLE 28

The provisions of the present Covenant shall extend to all parts of federal States without any limitations or exceptions.

ARTICLE 29

1. Any State Party to the present Covenant may propose an amendment and file it with the Secretary-General of the United Nations. The Secretary-General shall thereupon communicate any proposed amendments to the States Parties to the present Covenant with a request that they notify him whether they favour a conference of States Parties for the purpose of considering and voting upon the proposals. In the event that at least one-third of the States Parties favours such a conference, the Secretary-General shall convene the conference under the auspices of the United Nations. Any amendment adopted by a majority of the States Parties present and voting at the conference shall be submitted to the General Assembly of the United Nations for approval.

2. Amendments shall come into force when they have been approved by the General Assembly of the United Nations and accepted by a two-thirds majority of the States Parties to the present Covenant in accordance with their respective constitutional processes.

3. When amendments come into force they shall be binding on those States Parties which have accepted them, other States Parties still being bound by the provisions of the present Covenant and any earlier amendment which they have accepted.

ARTICLE 30

Irrespective of the notifications made under article 26, paragraph 5, the Secretary-General of the United Nations shall inform all States referred to in paragraph 1 of the same article of the following particulars:

(*a*) Signatures, ratifications and accessions under article 26;

(*b*) The date of the entry into force of the present Covenant under article 27 and the date of the entry into force of any amendments under article 29.

ARTICLE 31

1. The present Covenant, of which the Chinese, English, French, Russian and Spanish texts are equally authentic, shall be deposited in the archives of the United Nations.

2. The Secretary-General of the United Nations shall transmit certified copies of the present Covenant to all States referred to in article 26.

INTERNATIONAL COVENANT ON CIVIL AND POLITICAL RIGHTS

PREAMBLE

The States Parties to the present Covenant,

Considering that, in accordance with the principles proclaimed in the Charter of the United Nations, recognition of the inherent dignity and of the equal and inalienable rights of all members of the human family is the foundation of freedom, justice and peace in the world,

Recognizing that these rights derive from the inherent dignity of the human person,

Recognizing that, in accordance with the Universal Declaration of Human Rights, the ideal of free human beings enjoying civil and political freedom and freedom from fear and want can only be achieved if conditions are created whereby everyone may enjoy his civil and political rights, as well as his economic, social and cultural rights,

Considering the obligation of States under the Charter of the United Nations to promote universal respect for, and observance of, human rights and freedoms,

Realizing that the individual, having duties to other individuals and to the community to which he belongs, is under a responsibility to strive for the promotion and observance of the rights recognized in the present Covenant,

Agree upon the following articles:

PART I
ARTICLE 1

1. All peoples have the right of self-determination. By virtue of that right they freely determine their political status and freely pursue their economic, social and cultural development.

2. All peoples may, for their own ends, freely dispose of their natural wealth and resources without prejudice to any obligations arising out of international economic co-operation, based upon the principle of mutual benefit, and international law. In no case may a people be deprived of its own means of subsistence.

3. The States Parties to the present Covenant, including those having responsibility for the administration of Non-Self-Governing and Trust

Territories, shall promote the realization of the right of self-determination, and shall respect that right, in conformity with the provisions of the Charter of the United Nations.

PART II
ARTICLE 2

1. Each State Party to the present Covenant undertakes to respect and to ensure to all individuals within its territory and subject to its jurisdiction the rights recognized in the present Covenant, without distinction of any kind, such as race, colour, sex, language, religion, political or other opinion, national or social origin, property, birth or other status.

2. Where not already provided for by existing legislative or other measures, each State Party to the present Covenant undertakes to take the necessary steps, in accordance with its constitutional processes and with the provisions of the present Covenant, to adopt such legislative or other measures as may be necessary to give effect to the rights recognized in the present Covenant.

3. Each State Party to the present Covenant undertakes:

(*a*) To ensure that any person whose rights or freedoms as herein recognised are violated shall have an effective remedy, notwithstanding that the violation has been committed by persons acting in an official capacity;

(*b*) To ensure that any person claiming such a remedy shall have his right thereto determined by competent judicial, administrative or legislative authorities or by any other competent authority provided for by the legal system of the State, and to develop the possibilities of judicial remedy;

(*c*) To ensure that the competent authorities shall enforce such remedies when granted.

ARTICLE 3

The States Parties to the present Covenant undertake to ensure the equal right of men and women to the enjoyment of all civil and political rights set forth in the present Covenant.

ARTICLE 4

1. In time of public emergency which threatens the life of the nation and the existence of which is officially proclaimed, the States Parties to the present Covenant may take measures derogating from their obligations under the present Covenant to the extent strictly required by the exigencies of the situation, provided that such measures are not inconsistent with their other obligations under international law and do not involve discrimination solely on the ground of race, colour, sex, language, religion or social origin.

2. No derogation from articles 6, 7, 8 (paragraphs 1 and 2), 11, 15, 16 and 18 may be made under this provision.

3. Any State Party to the present Covenant availing itself of the right of derogation shall immediately inform the other States Parties to the present Covenant, through the intermediary of the Secretary-General of the United Nations, of the provisions from which it has derogated and of the reasons by which it was actuated. A further communication shall be made, through the same intermediary, on the date on which it terminates such derogation.

ARTICLE 5

1. Nothing in the present Covenant may be interpreted as implying for any State, group or person any right to engage in any activity or perform any act aimed at the destruction of any of the rights and freedoms recognized herein or at their limitation to a greater extent than is provided for in the present Covenant.

2. There shall be no restriction upon or derogation from any of the fundamental human rights recognized or existing in any State Party to the present Covenant pursuant to law, conventions, regulations or custom on the pretext that the present Covenant does not recognize such rights or that it recognizes them to a lesser extent.

PART III

ARTICLE 6

1. Every human being has the inherent right to life. This right shall be protected by law. No one shall be arbitrarily deprived of his life.

2. In countries which have not abolished the death penalty, sentence of death may be imposed only for the most serious crimes in accordance with the law in force at the time of the commission of the crime and not contrary to the provisions of the present Covenant and to the Convention on the Prevention and Punishment of the Crime of Genocide. This penalty can only be carried out pursuant to a final judgment rendered by a competent court.

3. When deprivation of life constitutes the crime of genocide, it is understood that nothing in this article shall authorize any State Party to the present Covenant to derogate in any way from any obligation assumed under the provisions of the Convention on the Prevention and Punishment of the Crime of Genocide.

4. Anyone sentenced to death shall have the right to seek pardon or commutation of the sentence. Amnesty, pardon or commutation of the sentence of death may be granted in all cases.

5. Sentence of death shall not be imposed for crimes committed by persons below eighteen years of age and shall not be carried out on pregnant women.

6. Nothing in this article shall be invoked to delay or to prevent the abolition of capital punishment by any State Party to the present Covenant.

ARTICLE 7

No one shall be subjected to torture or to cruel, inhuman or degrading treatment or punishment. In particular, no one shall be subjected without his free consent to medical or scientific experimentation.

ARTICLE 8

1. No one shall be held in slavery; slavery and the slave trade in all their forms shall be prohibited.

2. No one shall be held in servitude.

3. (*a*) No one shall be required to perform forced or compulsory labour;

   (*b*) Paragraph 3 (a) shall not be held to preclude, in countries where imprisonment with hard labour may be imposed as a punishment for a crime, the performance of hard labour in pursuance of a sentence to such punishment by a competent court;

(*b*) For the purpose of this paragraph the term 'forced or compulsory labour' shall not include:

  (i) Any work or service, not referred to in subparagraph (b), normally required of a person who is under detention in consequence of a lawful order of a court, or of a person during conditional release from such detention;

  (ii) any service of a military character and, in countries where conscientious objection is recognized, any national service required by law of conscientious objectors;

  (iii) Any service exacted in cases of emergency or calamity threatening the life or wellbeing of the community;

  (iv) Any work or service which forms part of normal civil obligations.

ARTICLE 9

1. Everyone has the right to liberty and security of person. No one shall be subjected to arbitrary arrest or detention. No one shall be deprived of his liberty except on such grounds and in accordance with such procedure as are established by law.

2. Anyone who is arrested shall be informed, at the time of arrest, of the reasons for his arrest and shall be promptly informed of any charges against him.

3. Anyone attested or detained on a criminal charge shall be brought promptly before a judge or other officer authorized by law to exercise judicial power and shall be entitled to trial within a reasonable time or to release. It shall not be the general rule that persons awaiting trial shall be detained in custody, but release may be subject to guarantees to appear for trial, at any other stage of the judicial proceedings, and, should occasion arise, for execution of the judgment.

4. Anyone who is deprived of his liberty by attest or detention shall be entitled to take proceedings before a court, in order that that court may decide without delay on the lawfulness of his detention and order his release if the detention is not lawful.

5. Anyone who has been the victim of unlawful arrest or detention shall have an enforceable right to compensation.

ARTICLE 10

1. All persons deprived of their liberty shall be treated with humanity and with respect for the inherent dignity of the human person.

2. (a) Accused persons shall, save in exceptional circumstances, be segregated from convicted persons and shall be subject to separate treatment appropriate to their status as unconvicted persons;

   (b) Accused juvenile persons shall be separated from adults and brought as speedily as possible for adjudication.

3. The penitentiary system shall comprise treatment of prisoners the essential aim of which shall be their reformation and social rehabilitation. Juvenile offenders shall be segregated from adults and be accorded treatment appropriate to their age and legal status.

ARTICLE 11

No one shall be imprisoned merely on the ground of inability to fulfil a contractual obligation.

ARTICLE 12

1. Everyone lawfully within the territory of a State shall, within that territory, have the right to liberty of movement and freedom to choose his residence.

2. Everyone shall be free to leave any country, including his own.

3. The above-mentioned rights shall not be subject to any restrictions except those which are provided by law, are necessary to protect national security, public order (*ordre public*), public health or morals or the rights and freedoms of others, and are consistent with the other rights recognized in the present Covenant.

4. No one shall be arbitrarily deprived of the right to enter his own country.

ARTICLE 13

An alien lawfully in the territory of a State Party to the present Covenant may be expelled therefrom only in pursuance of a decision reached in accordance with law and shall, except where compelling reasons of national security otherwise require, be allowed to submit the reasons against his expulsion and to have his case reviewed by, and be represented for the purpose before, the competent authority or a person or persons especially designated by the competent authority.

ARTICLE 14

1. All persons shall be equal before the courts and tribunals. In the determination of any criminal charge against him, or of his rights and obligations in a suit at law, everyone shall be entitled to a fair and public hearing by a competent, independent and impartial tribunal established by law. The Press and the public may be excluded from all or part of a trial for reasons of morals, public order (*ordre public*) or national security in a democratic society, or when the interest of the private lives of the parties so requires, or to the extent strictly necessary in the opinion of the court in special circumstances where publicity would prejudice the interests of justice; but any judgment rendered in a criminal case or in a suit at law shall be made public except where the interest of juvenile persons otherwise requires or the proceedings concern matrimonial disputes or the guardianship of children.

2. Everyone charged with a criminal offence shall have the right to be presumed innocent until proved guilty according to law.

3. In the determination of any criminal charge against him, everyone shall be entitled to the following minimum guarantees, in full equality:

    (*a*) To be informed promptly and in detail in a language which he understands of the nature and cause of the charge against him;

    (*b*) To have adequate time and facilities for the preparation of his defence and to communicate with counsel of his own choosing;

    (*c*) To be tried without undue delay;

    (*d*) To be tried in his presence, and to defend himself in person or through legal assistance of his own choosing; to be informed, if he does not have legal assistance, of this right; and to have legal assistance assigned to him, in any case where the interests of justice so require, and without payment by him in any such case if he does not have sufficient means to pay for it;

    (*e*) To examine, or have examined, the witnesses against him and to obtain the attendance and examination of witnesses on his behalf under the same conditions as witnesses against him;

(*f*) To have the free assistance of an interpreter if he cannot understand or speak the language used in court;

(*g*) Not to be compelled to testify against himself or to confess guilt.

4. In the case of juvenile persons, the procedure shall be such as will take account of their age and the desirability of promoting their rehabilitation.

5. Everyone convicted of a crime shall have the right to his conviction and sentence being reviewed by a higher tribunal according to law.

6. When a person has by a final decision been convicted of a criminal offence and when subsequently his conviction has been reversed or he has been pardoned on the ground that a new or newly discovered fact shows conclusively that there has been a miscarriage of justice, the person who has suffered punishment as a result of such conviction shall be compensated according to law, unless it is proved that the nondisclosure of the unknown fact in time is wholly or partly attributable to him.

7. No one shall be liable to be tried or punished again for an offence for which he has already been finally convicted or acquitted in accordance with the law and penal procedure of each country.

ARTICLE 15

1. No one shall be held guilty of any criminal offence on account of any act or omission which did not constitute a criminal offence, under national or international law, at the time when it was committed. Nor shall a heavier penalty be imposed than the one that was applicable at the time when the criminal offence was committed. If, subsequent to the commission of the offence, provision is made by law for the imposition of a lighter penalty, the offender shall benefit thereby.

2. Nothing in this article shall prejudice the trial and punishment of any person for any act or omission which, at the time when it was committed, was criminal according to the general principles of law recognized by the community of nations.

ARTICLE 16

Everyone shall have the right to recognition everywhere as a person before the law.

ARTICLE 17

1. No one shall be subjected to arbitrary or unlawful interference with his privacy, family, home or correspondence, nor to unlawful attacks on his honour and reputation.

2. Everyone has the right to the protection of the law against such interference or attacks.

ARTICLE 18

1. Everyone shall have the right to freedom of thought, conscience and religion. This right shall include freedom to have or to adopt a religion or belief of his choice, and freedom, either individually or in community with others and in public or private, to manifest his religion or belief in worship, observance, practice and teaching.

2. No one shall be subject to coercion which would impair his freedom to have or to adopt a religion or belief of his choice.

3. Freedom to manifest one's religion or beliefs may be subject only to such limitations as are prescribed by law and are necessary to protect public safety, order, health, or morals or the fundamental rights and freedoms of others.

4. The States Parties to the present Covenant undertake to have respect for the liberty of parents and, when applicable, legal guardians to ensure the religious and moral education of their children in conformity with their own convictions.

ARTICLE 19

1. Everyone shall have the right to hold opinions without interference.

2. Everyone shall have the right to freedom of expression; this right shall include freedom to seek, receive and impart information and ideas of all kinds, regardless of frontiers, either orally, in writing or in print, in the form of art, or through any other media of his choice.

3. The exercise of the rights provided for in paragraph 2 of this article carries with it special duties and responsibilities. It may therefore be subject to certain restrictions, but these shall only be such as are provided by law and are necessary:

(*a*) For respect of the rights or reputations of others;

(*b*) For the protection of national security or of public order (*ordre public*), or of public health or morals.

ARTICLE 20

1. Any propaganda for war shall be prohibited by law.

2. Any advocacy of national, racial or religious hatred that constitutes incitement to discrimination, hostility or violence shall be prohibited by law.

ARTICLE 21

The right of peaceful assembly shall be recognized. No restrictions may be placed on the exercise of this right other than those imposed in conformity with the law and which are necessary in a democratic society in the interests of national security or public safety, public order (*ordre public*), the protection of public health or morals or the protection of the rights and freedoms of others.

ARTICLE 22

1. Everyone shall have the right to freedom of association with others, including the right to form and join trade unions for the protection of his interests.

2. No restrictions may be placed on the exercise of this right other than those which are prescribed by law and which are necessary in a democratic society in the interests of national security or public safety, public order (*ordre public*), the protection of public health or morals or the protection of the rights and freedoms of others. This article shall not prevent the imposition of lawful restrictions on members of the armed forces and of the police in their exercise of this right.

3. Nothing in this article shall authorize States Parties to the International Labour Organisation Convention of 1948 concerning Freedom of Association and Protection of the Right to Organize to take legislative measures which would prejudice, or to apply the law in such a manner as to prejudice, the guarantees provided for in that Convention.

ARTICLE 23

1. The family is the natural and fundamental group unit of society and is entitled to protection by society and the State.

2. The right of men and women of marriageable age to marry and to found a family shall be recognized.

3. No marriage shall be entered into without the free and full consent of the intending spouses.

4. States Parties to the present Covenant shall take appropriate steps to ensure equality of rights and responsibilities of spouses as to marriage, during marriage and at its dissolution. In the case of dissolution, provision shall be made for the necessary protection of any children.

ARTICLE 24

1. Every child shall have, without any discrimination as to race, colour, sex, language, religion, national or social origin, property or birth, the right to such measures of protection as are required by his status as a minor, on the part of his family, society and the State.

2. Every child shall be registered immediately after birth and shall have a name.

3. Every child has the right to acquire a nationality.

ARTICLE 25

Every citizen shall have the right and the opportunity, without any of the distinctions mentioned in article 2 and without unreasonable restrictions:

(*a*) To take part in the conduct of public affairs, directly or through freely chosen representatives;

(*b*) To vote and to be elected at genuine periodic elections which shall be by universal and equal suffrage and shall be held by secret ballot, guaranteeing the free expression of the will of the electors;

(*c*) To have access, on general terms of equality, to public service in his country.

ARTICLE 26

All persons are equal before the law and are entitled without any discrimination to the equal protection of the law. In this respect, the law shall prohibit any discrimination and guarantee to all persons equal and effective protection against discrimination on any ground such as race, colour, sex, language, religion, political or other opinion, national or social origin, property, birth or other status.

ARTICLE 27

In those States in which ethnic, religious or linguistic minorities exist, persons belonging to such minorities shall not be denied the right, in community with the other members of their group, to enjoy their own culture, to profess and practise their own religion, or to use their own language.

PART IV
ARTICLE 28

1. There shall be established a Human Rights Committee (hereafter referred to in the present Covenant as the Committee). It shall consist of eighteen members and shall carry out the functions hereinafter provided.

2. The Committee shall be composed of nationals of the States Parties to the present Covenant who shall be persons of high moral character and recognized competence in the field of human rights, consideration being given to the usefulness of the participation of some persons having legal experience.

3. The members of the Committee shall be elected and shall serve in their personal capacity.

ARTICLE 29

1. The members of the Committee shall be elected by secret ballot from a list of persons possessing the qualifications prescribed in article 28 and nominated for the purpose by the States Parties to the present Covenant.

2. Each State Party to the present Covenant may nominate not more than two persons. These persons shall be nationals of the nominating State.

3. A person shall be eligible for renomination.

ARTICLE 30

1. The initial election shall be held no later than six months after the date of the entry into force of the present Covenant.

2. At least four months before the date of each election to the Committee, other than an election to fill a vacancy declared in accordance with article 34, the Secretary-General of the United Nations shall address a written invitation to the States Parties to the present Covenant to submit their nominations for membership of the Committee within three months.

3. The Secretary-General of the United Nations shall prepare a list in alphabetical order of all the persons thus nominated, with an indication of the States Parties which have nominated them, and shall submit it to the States Parties to the present Covenant no later than one month before the date of each election.

4. Elections of the members of the Committee shall be held at a meeting of the States Parties to the present Covenant convened by the Secretary-General of the United Nations at the Headquarters of the United Nations. At that meeting, for which two-thirds of the States Parties to the present Covenant shall constitute a quorum, the persons elected to the Committee shall be those nominees who obtain the largest number of votes and an absolute majority of the votes of the representatives of States Parties present and voting.

ARTICLE 31

1. The Committee may not include more than one national of the same State.

2. In the election of the Committee, consideration shall be given to equitable geographical distribution of membership and to the representation of the different forms of civilization and of the principal legal systems.

ARTICLE 32

1. The members of the Committee shall be elected for a term of four years. They shall be eligible for re-election if renominated. However, the terms of nine of the members elected at the first election shall expire at the end of two years; immediately after the first election, the names of these nine members shall be chosen by lot by the Chairman of the meeting referred to in article 30, paragraph 4.

2. Elections at the expiry of office shall be held in accordance with the preceding articles of this part of the present Covenant.

ARTICLE 33

1. If, in the unanimous opinion of the other members, a member of the Committee has ceased to carry out his functions for any cause other than absence of a temporary character, the Chairman of the Committee shall notify the Secretary-General of the United Nations, who shall then declare the seat of that member to be vacant.

2. In the event of the death or the resignation of a member of the Committee, the Chairman shall immediately notify the Secretary-General of the United Nations, who shall declare the seat vacant from the date of death or the date on which the resignation takes effect.

ARTICLE 34

1. When a vacancy is declared in accordance with article 33 and if the term of office of the member to be replaced does not expire within six months of the declaration of the vacancy, the Secretary-General of the United Nations shall notify each of the States Parties to the present Covenant, which may within two months submit nominations in accordance with article 29 for the purpose of filling the vacancy.

2. The Secretary-General of the United Nations shall prepare a list in alphabetical order of the persons thus nominated and shall submit it to the States Parties to the present Covenant. The election to fill the vacancy shall then take place in accordance with the relevant provisions of this part of the present Covenant.

3. A member of the Committee elected to fill a vacancy declared in accordance with article 33 shall hold office for the remainder of the term of the member who vacated the seat on the Committee under the provisions of that article.

ARTICLE 35

The members of the Committee shall, with the approval of the General Assembly of the United Nations, receive emoluments from United Nations resources on such terms and conditions as the General Assembly may decide, having regard to the importance of the Committee's responsibilities.

ARTICLE 36

The Secretary-General of the United Nations shall provide the necessary staff and facilities for the effective performance of the functions of the Committee under the present Covenant.

ARTICLE 37

1. The Secretary-General of the United Nations shall convene the initial meeting of the Committee at the Headquarters of the United Nations.

2. After its initial meeting, the Committee shall meet at such times as shall be provided in its rules of procedure.

3. The Committee shall normally meet at the Headquarters of the United Nations or at the United Nations Office at Geneva.

ARTICLE 38

Every member of the Committee shall, before taking up his duties, make a solemn declaration in open committee that he will perform his functions impartially and conscientiously.

ARTICLE 39

1. The Committee shall elect its officers for a term of two years. They may be re-elected.

2. The Committee shall establish its own rules of procedure, but these rules shall provide, inter alia, that:

(*a*) Twelve members shall constitute a quorum;

(*b*) Decisions of the Committee shall be made by a majority vote of the members present.

ARTICLE 40

1. The States Parties to the present Covenant undertake to submit reports on the measures they have adopted which give effect to the rights recognized herein and on the progress made in the enjoyment of those rights:

(*a*) Within one year of the entry into force of the present Covenant for the States Parties concerned;

(*b*) Thereafter whenever the Committee so requests.

2. All reports shall be submitted to the Secretary-General of the United Nations, who shall transmit them to the Committee for consideration. Reports shall indicate the factors and difficulties, if any, affecting the implementation of the present Covenant.

3. The Secretary-General of the United Nations may, after consultation with the Committee, transmit to the specialized agencies concerned copies of such parts of the reports as may fall within their field of competence.

4. The Committee shall study the reports submitted by the States Parties to the present Covenant. It shall transmit its reports, and such general comments as it may consider appropriate, to the States Parties. The Committee may also transmit to the Economic and Social Council these comments along with the copies of the reports it has received from States Parties to the present Covenant.

5. The States Parties to the present Covenant may submit to the Committee observations on any comments that may be made in accordance with paragraph 4 of this Article.

ARTICLE 41

1. A State Party to the present Covenant may at any time declare under this Article that it recognizes the competence of the Committee to receive and consider communications to the effect that a State Party claims that another State Party is not fulfilling its obligations under the present Covenant. Communications under this Article may be received and considered only if submitted by a State Party which has made a declaration recognizing in regard to itself the competence of the Committee. No communication shall be received by the Committee if it concerns a State Party which has not made such a declaration. Communications received under this Article shall be dealt with in accordance with the following procedure:

(*a*) If a State Party to the present Covenant considers that another State Party is not giving effect to the provisions of the present Covenant, it may, by written communication, bring the matter to the attention of that State Party. Within three months after the receipt of the communication, the receiving State shall afford the State which sent the communication an explanation or any other statement in writing clarifying the matter, which should include, to the extent possible and pertinent, reference to domestic procedures and remedies taken, pending, or available in the matter.

(*b*) If the matter is not adjusted to the satisfaction of both States Parties concerned within six months after the receipt by the receiving State of the initial communication, either State shall have the right to refer the matter to the Committee, by notice given to the Committee and to the other State.

(*c*) The Committee shall deal with a matter referred to it only after it has ascertained that all available domestic remedies have been invoked and exhausted in the matter, in conformity with the generally recognized principles of international law. This shall not be the rule where the application of the remedies is unreasonably prolonged.

(*d*) The Committee shall hold closed meetings when examining communications under this article.

(*e*) Subject to the provisions of subparagraph (c), the Committee shall make available its good offices to the States Parties concerned with a view to a friendly solution of the matter on the basis of respect for human rights and fundamental freedoms as recognised in the present Covenant.

(*f*) In any matter referred to it, the Committee may call upon the States Parties concerned, referred to in subparagraph (b), to supply any relevant information.

(*g*) The States Parties concerned, referred to in subparagraph (b), shall have the right to be represented when the matter is being considered in the Committee and to make submissions orally and/or in writing.

(*h*) The Committee shall, within twelve months after the date of receipt of notice under subparagraph (b), submit a report:

(i) If a solution within the terms of subparagraph (e) is reached, the Committee shall confine its report to a brief statement of the facts and of the solution reached;

(ii) If a solution within the terms of subparagraph (e) is not reached, the Committee shall confine its report to a brief statement of the facts; the written submissions and record of the oral submissions made by the States Parties concerned shall be attached to the report.

In every matter, the report shall be communicated to the States Parties concerned.

2. The provisions of this Article shall come into force when ten States Parties to the present Covenant have made declarations under paragraph 1 of this Article. Such declarations shall be deposited by the States Parties with the Secretary-General of the United Nations, who shall transmit copies thereof to the other States Parties. A declaration may be withdrawn at any time by notification to the Secretary-General. Such a withdrawal shall not prejudice the consideration of any matter which is the subject of a communication already transmitted under this Article; no further communication by any State Party shall be received after the notification of withdrawal of the declaration has been received by the Secretary-General unless the State Party concerned has made a new declaration.

ARTICLE 42

1. (*a*) If a matter referred to the Committee in accordance with article 41 is not resolved to the satisfaction of the States Parties concerned, the Committee may, with the prior consent of the States Parties concerned, appoint an ad hoc Conciliation Commission (hereinafter referred to as the Commission). The good offices of the Commission shall be made available to the States Parties concerned with a view to an amicable solution of the matter on the basis of respect for the present Covenant;

   (*b*) The Commission shall consist of five persons acceptable to the States Parties concerned. If the States Parties concerned fail to reach agreement within three months on all or part of the composition of the Commission the members of the Commission concerning whom no agreement has been reached shall be elected by secret ballot by a two-thirds majority vote of the Committee from among its members.

2. The members of the Commission shall serve in their personal capacity. They shall not be nationals of the States Parties concerned, or of a State not party to the present Covenant, or of a State Party which has not made a declaration under article 41.

3. The Commission shall elect its own Chairman and adopt its own rules of procedure.

4. The meetings of the Commission shall normally be held at the Headquarters of the United Nations or at the United Nations Office at Geneva. However, they may be held at such other convenient places as the Commission

may determine in consultation with the Secretary-General of the United Nations and the States Parties concerned.

5. The secretariat provided in accordance with Article 36 shall also service the commissions appointed under this article.

6. The information received and collated by the Committee shall be made available to the Commission and the Commission may call upon the States Parties concerned to supply any other relevant information.

7. When the Commission has fully considered the matter, but in any event not later than twelve months after having been seized of the matter, it shall submit to the Chairman of the Committee a report for communication to the States Parties concerned.

- (*a*) If the Commission is unable to complete its consideration of the matter within twelve months, it shall confine its report to a brief statement of the status of its consideration of the matter.

- (*b*) If an amicable solution to the matter on the basis of respect for human rights as recognized in the present Covenant is reached, the Commission shall confine its report to a brief statement of the facts and of the solution reached.

- (*c*) If a solution within the terms of subparagraph (b) is not reached, the Commission's report shall embody its findings on all questions of fact relevant to the issues between the States Parties concerned, and its views on the possibilities of an amicable solution of the matter. This report shall also contain the written submissions and a record of the oral submissions made by the States Parties concerned.

- (*d*) If the Commission's report is submitted under subparagraph (c), the States Parties concerned shall, within three months of the receipt of the report, notify the Chairman of the Committee whether or not they accept the contents of the report of the Commission.

8. The provisions of this Article are without prejudice to the responsibilities of the Committee under article 41.

9. The States Parties concerned shall share equally all the expenses of the members of the Commission in accordance with estimates to be provided by the Secretary-General of the United Nations.

10. The Secretary-General of the United Nations shall be empowered to pay the expenses of the members of the Commission, if necessary, before reimbursement by the States Parties concerned, in accordance with paragraph 9 of this article.

ARTICLE 43

The members of the Committee, and of the ad hoc conciliation commissions which may be appointed under article 42, shall be entitled to the facilities, privileges and immunities of experts on mission for the United Nations as laid down in the relevant sections of the Convention on the Privileges and Immunities of the United Nations.

ARTICLE 44

The provisions for the implementation of the present Covenant shall apply without prejudice to the procedures prescribed in the field of human rights by or under the constituent instruments and the conventions of the United Nations and of the specialized agencies and shall not prevent the States Parties to the present Covenant from having recourse to other procedures for settling a dispute in accordance with general or special international agreements in force between them.

ARTICLE 45

The Committee shall submit to the General Assembly of the United Nations, through the Economic and Social Council, an annual report on its activities.

PART V
ARTICLE 46

Nothing in the present Covenant shall be interpreted as impairing the provisions of the Charter of the United Nations and of the constitutions of the specialized agencies which define the respective responsibilities of the various organs of the United Nations and of the specialized agencies in regard to the matters dealt with in the present Covenant.

ARTICLE 47

Nothing in the present Covenant shall be interpreted as impairing the inherent right of all peoples to enjoy and utilize fully and freely their natural wealth and resources.

PART VI

ARTICLE 48

1. The present Covenant is open for signature by any State Member of the United Nations or member of any of its specialized agencies, by any State Party to the Statute of the International Court of Justice, and by any other State which has been invited by the General Assembly of the United Nations to become a party to the present Covenant.

2. The present Covenant is subject to ratification. Instruments of ratification shall be deposited with the Secretary-General of the United Nations.

3. The present Covenant shall be open to accession by any State referred to in paragraph 1 of this Article.

4. Accession shall be effected by the deposit of an instrument of accession with the Secretary-General of the United Nations.

5. The Secretary-General of the United Nations shall inform all States which have signed this Covenant or acceded to it of the deposit of each instrument of ratification or accession.

ARTICLE 49

1. The present Covenant shall enter into force three months after the date of the deposit with the Secretary-General of the United Nations of the thirty-fifth instrument of ratification or instrument of accession.

2. For each State ratifying the present Covenant or acceding to it after the deposit of the thirty-fifth instrument of ratification or instrument of accession, the present Covenant shall enter into force three months after the date of the deposit of its own instrument of ratification or instrument of accession.

ARTICLE 50

The provisions of the present Covenant shall extend to all parts of federal States without any limitations or exceptions.

ARTICLE 51

1. Any State Party to the present Covenant may propose an amendment and file it with the Secretary-General of the United Nations. The Secretary-General of the United Nations shall thereupon communicate any proposed amendments to the States Parties to the present Covenant with a request that they notify him whether they favour a conference of States Parties for the purpose of considering and voting upon the proposals. In the event that at least one-third of the States Parties favours such a conference, the Secretary-General shall convene the conference under the auspices of the United Nations. Any amendment adopted by a majority of the States Parties present and voting at the conference shall be submitted to the General Assembly of the United Nations for approval.

2. Amendments shall come into force when they have been approved by the General Assembly of the United Nations and accepted by a two-thirds majority of the States Parties to the present Covenant in accordance with their respective constitutional processes.

3. When amendments come into force, they shall be binding on those States Parties which have accepted them, other States Parties still being bound by the provisions of the present Covenant and any earlier amendment which they have accepted.

ARTICLE 52

Irrespective of the notifications made under article 48, paragraph 5, the Secretary-General of the United Nations shall inform all States referred to in paragraph 1 of the same article of the following particulars:

(*a*) Signatures, ratifications and accessions under article 48;

(*b*) The date of the entry into force of the present Covenant under article 49 and the date of the entry into force of any amendments under article 51.

ARTICLE 53

1. The present Covenant, of which the Chinese, English, French, Russian and Spanish texts are equally authentic, shall be deposited in the archives of the United Nations.

2. The Secretary-General of the United Nations shall transmit certified copies of the present Covenant to all States referred to in article 48.

OPTIONAL PROTOCOL TO THE INTERNATIONAL COVENANT ON CIVIL AND POLITICAL RIGHTS

The States Parties to the present Protocol,

Considering that in order further to achieve the purposes of the Covenant on Civil and Political Rights (hereinafter referred to as the Covenant) and the implementation of its provisions it would be appropriate to enable the Human Rights Committee set up in part IV of the Covenant (hereinafter referred to as the Committee) to receive and consider, as provided in the present Protocol, communications from individuals claiming to be victims of violations of any of the rights set forth in the Covenant,

Have agreed as follows:

ARTICLE 1

A State Party to the Covenant that becomes a party to the present Protocol recognises the competence of the Committee to receive and consider communications from individuals subject to its jurisdiction who claim to be victims of a violation by that State Party of any of the rights set forth in the Covenant. No communication shall be received by the Committee if it concerns a State Party to the Covenant which is not a party to the present Protocol.

ARTICLE 2

Subject to the provisions of article 1, individuals who claim that any of their rights enumerated in the Covenant have been violated and who have exhausted all available domestic remedies may submit a written communication to the Committee for consideration.

ARTICLE 3

The Committee shall consider inadmissible any communication under the present Protocol which is anonymous, or which it considers to be an abuse of the right of submission of such communications or to be incompatible with the provisions of the Covenant.

ARTICLE 4

1. Subject to the provisions of article 3, the Committee shall bring any communications submitted to it under the present Protocol to the attention of the State Party to the present Protocol alleged to be violating any provision of the Covenant.

2. Within six months, the receiving State shall submit to the Committee written explanations or statements clarifying the matter and the remedy, if any, that may have been taken by that State.

ARTICLE 5

1. The Committee shall consider communications received under the present Protocol in the light of all written information made available to it by the individual and by the State Party concerned.

2. The Committee shall not consider any communication from an individual unless it has ascertained that:

(*a*) The same matter is not being examined under another procedure of international investigation or settlement;

(*b*) The individual has exhausted all available domestic remedies.

This shall not be the rule where the application of the remedies is unreasonably prolonged.

3. The Committee shall hold closed meetings when examining communications under the present Protocol.

4. The Committee shall forward its views to the State Party concerned and to the individual.

ARTICLE 6

The Committee shall include in its annual report under article 45 of the Covenant a summary of its activities under the present Protocol.

ARTICLE 7

Pending the achievement of the objectives of resolution 1514 (XV) adopted by the General Assembly of the United Nations on 14 December 1960 concerning the Declaration on the Granting of Independence to Colonial Countries and Peoples, the provisions of the present Protocol shall in no way limit the right of petition granted to these peoples by the Charter of the United Nations and other international conventions and instruments under the United Nations and its specialized agencies.

ARTICLE 8

1. The present Protocol is open for signature by any State which has signed the Covenant.

2. The present Protocol is subject to ratification by any State which has ratified or acceded to the Covenant. Instruments of ratification shall be deposited with the Secretary-General of the United Nations.

3. The present Protocol shall be open to accession by any State which has ratified or acceded to the Covenant.

4. Accession shall be effected by the deposit of an instrument of accession with the Secretary-General of the United Nations.

5. The Secretary-General of the United Nations shall inform all States which have signed the present Protocol or acceded to it of the deposit of each instrument of ratification or accession.

ARTICLE 9

1. Subject to the entry into force of the Covenant, the present Protocol shall enter into force three months after the date of the deposit with the Secretary-General of the United Nations of the tenth instrument of ratification or instrument of accession.

2. For each State ratifying the present Protocol or acceding to it after the deposit of the tenth instrument of ratification, or instrument of accession, the present Protocol shall enter into force three months after the date of the deposit of its own instrument of ratification or instrument of accession.

ARTICLE 10

The provisions of the present Protocol shall extend to all parts of federal States without any limitations or exceptions.

ARTICLE 11

1. Any State Party to the present Protocol may propose an amendment and file it with the Secretary-General of the United Nations. The Secretary-General shall thereupon communicate any proposed amendments to the States Parties to the present Protocol with a request that they notify him whether they favour a conference of States Parties for the purpose of considering and voting upon the proposal. In the event that at least one-third of the States Parties favours such a conference, the Secretary-General shall convene the conference under the auspices of the United Nations. Any amendment adopted by a majority of the States Parties present and voting at the conference shall be submitted to the General Assembly of the United Nations for approval.

2. Amendments shall come into force when they have been approved by the General Assembly of the United Nations and accepted by a two-thirds majority of the States Parties to the present Protocol in accordance with their respective constitutional processes.

3. When amendments come into force, they shall be binding on those States Parties which have accepted them, other States Parties still being bound by the provisions of the present Protocol and any earlier amendment which they have accepted.

ARTICLE 12

1. Any State Party may denounce the present Protocol at any time by written notification addressed to the Secretary-General of the United Nations. Denunciation shall take effect three months alter the date of receipt of the notification by the Secretary-General.

2. Denunciation shall be without prejudice to the continued application of the provisions of the present Protocol to any communication submitted under article 2 before the effective date of denunciation.

ARTICLE 13

Irrespective of the notifications made under article 8, paragraph 5, of the present Protocol, the Secretary-General of the United Nations shall inform all States referred to in article 48, paragraph 1, of the Covenant of the following particulars:

(*a*) Signatures, ratifications and accessions under article 8;

(*b*) The date of the entry into force of the present Protocol under article 9 and the date of the entry into force of any amendments under article 11;

(*c*) Denunciations under article 12.

ARTICLE 14

1. The present Protocol, of which the Chinese, English, French, Russian and Spanish texts are equally authentic, shall be deposited in the archives of the United Nations.

2. The Secretary-General of the United Nations shall transmit certified copies of the present Protocol to all States referred to in article 48 of the Covenant.

EUROPEAN CONVENTION FOR THE PROTECTION OF HUMAN RIGHTS AND FUNDAMENTAL FREEDOMS

ARTICLE 1

The High Contracting Parties shall secure to everyone within their jurisdiction the rights and freedoms defined in Section I of this Convention.

SECTION I

ARTICLE 2

(1) Everyone's right to life shall be protected by law. No one shall be deprived of his life intentionally save in the execution of a sentence of a court following his conviction of a crime for which this penalty is provided by law.

(2) Deprivation of life shall not be regarded as inflicted in contravention of this Article when it results from the use of force which is no more than absolutely necessary—

    (*a*) in defence of any person from unlawful violence;

    (*b*) in order to effect a lawful arrest or to prevent the escape of a person lawfully detained;

    (*c*) in action lawfully taken for the purpose of quelling a riot or insurrection.

ARTICLE 3

No one shall be subjected to torture or to inhuman or degrading treatment or punishment.

ARTICLE 4

(1) No one shall be held in slavery or servitude.

(2) No one shall be required to perform forced or compulsory labour.

(3) For the purpose of this Article the term 'forced or compulsory labour' shall not include—

(*a*) any work required to be done in the ordinary course of detention imposed according to the provisions of article 5 of this Convention or during conditional release from such detention;

(*b*) any service of a military character or, in the case of conscientious objectors in countries where they are recognised, service exacted instead of compulsory military service;

(*c*) any service exacted in case of an emergency or calamity threatening the life or wellbeing of the community;

(*d*) any work or service which forms part of normal civic obligations.

ARTICLE 5

(1) Everyone has the right to liberty and security of person. No one shall be deprived of his liberty save in the following cases and in accordance with a procedure prescribed by law.

(*a*) the lawful detention of a person after conviction by a competent court;

(*b*) the lawful arrest or detention of a person for non-compliance with the lawful order of a court or in order to secure the fulfilment of any obligation prescribed by law;

(*c*) the lawful arrest or detention of a person effected for the purpose of bringing him before the competent legal authority on reasonable suspicion of having committed an offence or when it is reasonably considered necessary to prevent his committing an offence or fleeing after having done so;

(*d*) the detention of a minor by lawful order for the purpose of educational supervision or his lawful detention for the purpose of bringing him before the competent legal authority;

(*e*) the lawful detention of persons for the prevention of the spreading of infectious diseases, of persons of unsound mind, alcoholics or drug addicts or vagrants;

(*f*) the lawful arrest or detention of a person to prevent his effecting an unauthorised entry into the country or of a person against whom action is being taken with a view to deportation or extradition.

(2) Everyone who is arrested shall be informed promptly, in a language which he understands, of the reasons for his arrest and of any charge against him.

(3) Everyone arrested or detained in accordance with the provisions of paragraph 1 (c) of this Article shall be bought promptly before a judge or other officer authorised by law to exercise judicial power and shall be entitled to trial within a reasonable time to release pending trial. Release may be conditioned by guarantees to appear for trial.

(4) Everyone who is deprived of his liberty by arrest or detention shall be entitled to take proceedings by which the lawfulness of his detention shall be decided speedily by a court and his release ordered if the detention is not lawful.

(5) Everyone who has been the victim of arrest or detention in contravention of the provisions of this Article shall have an enforceable right to compensation.

ARTICLE 6

(1) In the determination of his civil rights and obligations or of any, criminal charge against him, everyone is entitled to a fair and public hearing within a reasonable time by an independent and impartial tribunal established by law. Judgment shall be pronounced publicly but the press and public may be excluded from all or part of the trial in the interests of morals, public order or national security in a democratic society, where the interests of juveniles or the protection of the private life of the parties so require, or to the extent strictly necessary in the opinion of the court in special circumstances where publicity would prejudice the interests of justice.

(2) Everyone charged with a criminal offence shall be presumed innocent until proved guilty according to law.

(3) Everyone charged with a criminal offence has the following minimum rights:

(*a*) to be informed promptly, in a language which he understands and in detail, of the nature and cause of the accusation against him;

(*b*) to have adequate time and facilities for the preparation of his defence;

(*c*) to defend himself in person or through legal assistance of his own choosing or, if he has not sufficient means to pay for legal assistance, to be given it free when the interests of justice so require;

(*d*) to examine or have examined witnesses against him and to obtain the attendance and examination of witnesses on his behalf under the same conditions as witnesses against him;

(*e*) to have the free assistance of an interpreter if he cannot understand or speak the language used in court.

ARTICLE 7

(1) No one shall be held guilty of any criminal offence on account of any act or omission which did not constitute a criminal offence under national or international law at the time when it was committed. Nor shall a heavier penalty be imposed than the one that was applicable at the time the criminal offence was committed.

(2) This Article shall not prejudice the trial and punishment of any person for any act or omission which, at the time when it was committed, was criminal according to the general principles of law recognised by civilised nations.

ARTICLE 8

(1) Everyone has the right to respect for his private and family life, his home and his correspondence.

(2) There shall be no interference by a public authority with the exercise of this right except such as is in accordance with the law and is necessary in a democratic society in the interests of national security, public safety or the economic wellbeing of the country, for the prevention of disorder or crime, for the protection of health or morals, or for the protection of the rights and freedoms of others.

ARTICLE 9

(1) Everyone has the right to freedom of thought, conscience and religion; this right includes freedom to change his religion or belief and freedom, either alone or in community with others and, in public or private, to manifest his religion or belief, in worship, teaching, practice and observance.

(2) Freedom to manifest one's religion or beliefs shall be subject only to such limitations as are prescribed by law and are necessary in a democratic society in the

interests of public safety, for the protection of public order, health or morals, or for the protection of the rights and freedoms of others.

ARTICLE 10

(1) Everyone has the right to freedom of expression. This right shall include freedom to hold opinions and to receive and impart information and ideas without interference by public authority and regardless of frontiers. This Article shall not prevent States from requiring the licensing of broadcasting, television or cinema enterprises.

(2) The exercise of these freedoms, since it carries with it duties and responsibilities, may be subject to such formalities, conditions, restrictions or penalties as are prescribed by law and are necessary in a democratic society, in the interests of national security, territorial integrity or public safety, for the prevention of disorder or crime, for the protection of health or morals, for the protection of the reputation or rights of others, for preventing the disclosure of information received in confidence, or for maintaining the authority and impartiality of the judiciary.

ARTICLE 11

(1) Everyone has the right to freedom of peaceful assembly and to freedom of association with others, including the right to form and to join trade unions for the protection of his interests.

(2) No restrictions shall be placed on the exercise of these rights other than such as are prescribed by law and are necessary in a democratic society in the interests of national security or public safety, for the prevention of disorder or crime, for the protection of health or morals or for the protection of the rights and freedoms of others. This Article shall not prevent the imposition of lawful restrictions on the exercise of these rights by members of the armed forces, of the police or of the administration of the State.

ARTICLE 12

Men and women of marriageable age have the right to marry and to found a family, according to the national laws governing the exercise of this right.

ARTICLE 13

Everyone whose rights and freedoms as set forth in this Convention are violated shall have an effective remedy before a national authority notwithstanding that the violation has been committed by persons acting in an official capacity.

ARTICLE 14

The enjoyment of the rights and freedoms set forth in this Convention shall be secured without discrimination on any ground such as sex, race, colour, language, religion, political or other opinion, national or social origin, association with a national minority, property, birth or other status.

ARTICLE 15

(1) In time of war or other public emergency threatening the life of the nation any High Contracting Party may take measures derogating from its obligations under this Convention to the extent strictly required by the exigencies of the situation, provided that such measures are not inconsistent with its other obligations under international law.

(2) No derogation from article 2, except in respect of deaths resulting from lawful acts of war, or from articles 3, 4 (paragraph 1) and 7 shall be made under this provision.

(3) Any High Contracting Party availing itself of this right of derogation shall keep the Secretary-General of the Council of Europe fully informed of the measures which it has taken and the reasons therefore. It shall also inform the Secretary-General of the Council of Europe when such measures have ceased to operate and the provisions of the Convention are again being fully executed.

ARTICLE 16

Nothing in articles 10, 11 and 14 shall be regarded as preventing the High Contracting Parties from imposing restrictions on the political activity of aliens.

ARTICLE 17

Nothing in this Convention may be interpreted as implying for any State, group or person any right to engage in any activity or perform any act aimed at the destruction of any of the rights and freedoms set forth herein or at their limitation to a greater extent than is provided for in the Convention.

ARTICLE 18

The restrictions permitted under this Convention to the said rights and freedoms shall not be applied for any purpose other than those for which they have been prescribed.

SECTION II
ARTICLE 19

To ensure the observance of the engagements undertaken by the High Contracting Parties in the present Convention, there shall be set up

(1) A European Commission of Human Rights, hereinafter referred to as 'the Commission';

(2) A European Court of Human Rights, hereinafter referred to as 'the Court'.

SECTION III
ARTICLE 20

The Commission shall consist of a number of members equal to that of the High Contracting Parties. No two members of the Commission may be nationals of the same State.

ARTICLE 21

(1) The members of the Commission shall be elected by the Committee of Ministers by an absolute majority of votes, from a list of names drawn up by the Bureau of the Consultative Assembly; each group of the Representatives of the High Contracting Parties in the Consultative Assembly shall put forward three candidates, of whom two at least shall be its nationals.

(2) As far as applicable, the procedure shall be followed to complete the Commission in the event of other States subsequently becoming Parties to this Convention, and in filling casual vacancies.

ARTICLE 22

(1) The members of the Commission shall be elected for a period of six years. They may be re-elected. However, of the members elected at the first election, the terms of seven members shall expire at the end of three years.

(2) The members whose terms are to expire at the end of the initial period of three years shall be chosen by lot by the Secretary-General of the Council of Europe immediately after the first election has been completed.

(3) A member of the Commission elected to replace a member whose term of office has not expired shall hold office for the remainder of his predecessor's term.

(4) The members of the Commission shall hold office until replaced. After having been replaced, they shall continue to deal with such cases as they already have under consideration.

ARTICLE 23

The members of the Commission shall sit on the Commission in their individual capacity.

ARTICLE 24

Any High Contracting Party may refer to the Commission, through the Secretary-General of the Council of Europe, any alleged breach of the provisions of the Convention by another High Contracting Party.

ARTICLE 25

(1) The Commission may receive petitions addressed to the Secretary-General of the Council of Europe from any person, non-governmental organisation or group of individuals claiming to be the victim of a violation by one of the High Contracting Parties of the rights set forth in this Convention, provided that the High Contracting Party against which the complaint has been lodged has declared that it recognises the competence of the Commission to receive such petitions. Those of the High Contracting Parties who have made such a declaration undertake not to hinder in any way the effective exercise of this right.

(2) Such declarations may be made for a specific period.

(3) The declarations shall be deposited with the Secretary-General of the Council of Europe who shall transmit copies thereof to the High Contracting Parties and publish them.

(4) The Commission shall only exercise the powers provided for in this Article when at least six High Contracting Parties are bound by declarations made in accordance with the preceding paragraphs.

ARTICLE 26

The Commission may only deal with the matter after all domestic remedies have been exhausted, according to the generally recognised rules of international law, and within a period of six months from the date on which the final decision was taken.

ARTICLE 27

(1) The Commission shall not deal with any petition submitted under article 25 which—

(*a*) is anonymous, or

(*b*) is substantially the same as a matter which has already been examined by the Commission or has already been submitted to another procedure of international investigation or settlement and if it contains no relevant new information.

(2) The Commission shall consider inadmissible any petition submitted under article 25 which it considers incompatible with the provisions of the present Convention, manifestly ill-founded, or an abuse of the right petition.

(3) The Commission shall reject any petition referred to it which it considers inadmissible under article 26.

ARTICLE 28

In the event of the Commission accepting a petition referred to it—

(*a*) it shall, with a view to ascertaining the facts, undertake, together with the representatives of the parties, an examination of the petition and, if need be, an investigation, for the effective conduct of which the States concerned shall furnish all necessary facilities, after an exchange of views with the Commission;

(*b*) it shall place itself at the disposal of the parties concerned with a view to securing a friendly settlement of the matter on the basis of respect for Human Rights as defined in this Convention.

ARTICLE 29

(1) The Commission shall perform the functions set out in article 28 by means of a Sub-Commission consisting of seven members of the Commission.

(2) Each of the parties concerned may appoint as members of this Sub-Commission a person of its choice.

(3) The remaining members shall be chosen by lot in accordance with arrangements prescribed in the Rules of Procedure of the Commission.

ARTICLE 30

If the Sub-Commission succeeds in effecting a friendly settlement in accordance with article 28, it shall draw up a Report which shall be sent to the States concerned, to the Committee of Ministers and to the Secretary-General of the Council of Europe for publication. This Report shall be confined to a brief statement of the facts and of the solution reached.

ARTICLE 31

(1) If a solution is not reached, the Commission shall draw up a Report on the facts and state its opinion as to whether the facts found disclose a breach by the State concerned of its obligations under the Convention. The opinions of all the members of the Commission on this point may be stated in the Report.

(2) The Report shall be transmitted to the Committee of Ministers. It shall also be transmitted to the States concerned, who shall not be at liberty to publish it.

(3) In transmitting the Report to the Committee of Ministers the Commission may make such proposals as it thinks fit.

ARTICLE 32

(1) If the question is not referred to the Court in accordance with article 48 of this Convention within a period of three months from the date of the transmission of the Report to the Committee of Ministers, the Committee of Ministers shall decide by a majority of two-thirds of the members entitled to sit on the Committee whether there has been a violation of the Convention.

(2) In the affirmative case the Committee of Ministers shall prescribe a period during which the High Contracting Party concerned must take the measures required by the decision of the Committee of Ministers.

(3) If the High Contracting Party concerned has not taken satisfactory measures within the prescribed period, the Committee of Ministers shall decide by the majority provided for in paragraph (1) above what effect shall be given to its original decision and shall publish the Report.

(4) The High Contracting Parties undertake to regard as binding on them any decision which the Committee of Ministers may take in application of the preceding paragraphs.

ARTICLE 33

The Commission shall meet *in camera*.

ARTICLE 34

The Commission shall take its decisions by a majority of the Members present and voting; the Sub-Commission shall take its decisions by a majority of its members.

ARTICLE 35

The Commission shall meet as the circumstances require. The meetings shall be convened by the Secretary-General of the Council of Europe.

ARTICLE 36

The Commission shall draw up its own rules of procedure.

ARTICLE 37

The secretariat of the Commission shall be provided by the Secretary-General of the Council of Europe.

SECTION IV
ARTICLE 38

The European Court of Human Rights shall consist of a number of judges equal to that of the Members of the Council of Europe. No two judges may be nationals of the same State.

ARTICLE 39

(1) The members of the Court shall be elected by the Consultative Assembly by a majority of the votes cast from a list of persons nominated by the Members of the Council of Europe; each Member shall nominate three candidates of whom two at least shall be its nationals.

(2) As far as applicable, the same procedure shall be followed to complete the Court in the event of the admission of new Members of the Council of Europe, and in filling casual vacancies.

(3) The candidates shall be of high moral character and must either possess the qualifications required for appointment to high judicial office or be jurisconsults of recognised competence.

ARTICLE 40

(1) The members of the Court shall be elected for a period of nine years. They may be re-elected. However, of the members elected at the first election the terms of four members shall expire at the end of three years and the terms of four more members shall expire at the end of six years.

(2) The members whose terms are to expire at the end of the initial periods of three and six years shall be chosen by lot by the Secretary-General immediately after the first election has been completed.

(3) A member of the Court elected to replace a member whose term of office has not expired shall hold office for the remainder of his predecessor's term.

(4) The members of the Court shall hold office until replaced. After having been replaced, they shall continue to deal with such cases as they already have under consideration.

ARTICLE 41

The Court shall elect its President and Vice-President for a period of three years. They may be re-elected.

ARTICLE 42

The members of the Court shall receive for each day of duty a compensation to be determined by the Committee of Ministers.

ARTICLE 43

For the consideration of each case brought before it the Court shall consist of a Chamber composed of seven judges. There shall sit as an *ex officio* member of the Chamber the judge who is a national of any State party concerned, or, if there is none, a person of its choice who shall sit in the capacity of judge; the names of the other judges shall be chosen by lot by the President before the opening of the case.

ARTICLE 44

Only the High Contracting Parties and the Commission shall have the right to bring a case before the Court.

ARTICLE 45

The jurisdiction of the Court shall extend to all cases concerning the interpretation and application of the present Convention which the High Contracting Parties or the Commission shall refer to it in accordance with article 48.

ARTICLE 46

(1) Any of the High Contracting Parties may at any time declare that it recognises as compulsory *ipso facto* and without special agreement the jurisdiction

of the Court in all matters concerning the interpretation and application of the present Convention.

(2) The declaration referred to above may be made unconditionally or on condition of reciprocity on the part of several or certain other High Contracting Parties or for a specified period.

(3) These declarations shall be deposited with the Secretary-General of the Council of Europe who shall transmit copies thereof to the High Contracting Parties.

ARTICLE 47

The Court may only deal with a case after the Commission has acknowledged the failure of efforts for a friendly settlement and within the period of three months provided for in article 32.

ARTICLE 48

The following may bring a case before the Court, provided that the High Contracting Party concerned, if there is only one, or the High Contracting Parties concerned, if there is more than one, are subject to the compulsory jurisdiction of the Court or, failing that, with the consent of the High Contracting Party concerned, if there is only one, or of the High Contracting Parties concerned if there is more than one—

    (*a*) the Commission;

    (*b*) a High Contracting Party whose national is alleged to be a victim;

    (*c*) a High Contracting Party which referred the case to the Commission;

    (*d*) a High Contracting Party against which the complaint has been lodged.

ARTICLE 49

In the event of dispute as to whether the Court has jurisdiction, the matter shall be settled by the decision of the Court.

ARTICLE 50

If the Court finds that a decision or a measure taken by a legal authority or any other authority of a High Contracting Party is completely or partially in conflict with the obligations arising from the present Convention, and if the internal law of the said Party allows only partial reparation to be made for the consequences of this decision or measure, the decision of the Court shall, if necessary, afford just satisfaction to the injured party.

ARTICLE 51

(1) Reasons shall be given for the judgment of the Court.

(2) If the judgment does not represent in whole or in part the unanimous opinion of the judges, any judge shall be entitled to deliver a separate opinion.

ARTICLE 52

The judgment of the Court shall be final.

ARTICLE 53

The High Contracting Parties undertake to abide by the decision of the Court in any case to which they are parties.

ARTICLE 54

The judgment of the Court shall be transmitted to the Committee of Ministers which shall supervise its execution.

ARTICLE 55

The Court shall draw up its own rules and shall determine its own procedure.

ARTICLE 56

(1) The first election of the members of the Court shall take place after the declarations by the High Contracting Parties mentioned in article 46 have reached a total of eight.

(2) No case can be brought before the Court before this election.

SECTION V

ARTICLE 57

On receipt of a request from the Secretary-General of the Council of Europe any High Contracting Party shall furnish an explanation of the manner in which its internal law ensures the effective implementation of any of the provisions of this Convention.

ARTICLE 58

The expenses of the Commission and the Court shall be borne by the Council of Europe.

ARTICLE 59

The members of the Commission and of the Court shall be entitled, during the discharge of their functions, to the privileges and immunities provided for in article 40 of the Statute of the Council of Europe and in the agreements made thereunder.

ARTICLE 60

Nothing in this Convention shall be construed as limiting or derogating from any of the human rights and fundamental freedoms which may be ensured under the laws of any High Contracting Party or under any other agreement to which it is a Party.

ARTICLE 61

Nothing in this Convention shall prejudice the powers conferred on the Committee of Ministers by the Statute of the Council of Europe.

ARTICLE 62

The High Contracting Parties agree that, except by special agreement, they will not avail themselves of treaties, conventions or declarations in force between them for the purpose of submitting, by way of petition, a dispute arising out of the interpretation or application of this Convention to a means of settlement other than those provided for in this Convention.

ARTICLE 63

(1) Any State may at the time of its ratification or at any time thereafter declare by notification addressed to the Secretary-General of the Council of Europe that the present Convention shall extend to all or any of the territories for whose international relations it is responsible.

(2) The Convention shall extend to the territory or territories named in the notification as from the thirtieth day after the receipt of this notification by the Secretary-General of the Council of Europe.

(3) The provisions of this Convention shall be applied in such territories with due regard, however, to local requirements.

(4) Any State which has made a declaration in accordance with paragraph 1 of this article may at any time thereafter declare on behalf of one or more of the territories to which the declaration relates that it accepts the competence of the Commission to receive petitions from individuals, non-governmental organisations or groups of individuals in accordance with article 25 of the present Convention.

ARTICLE 64

(1) Any State may, when signing this Convention or when depositing its instrument of ratification, make a reservation in respect of any particular provision of the Convention to the extent that any law then in force in its territory is not in conformity with the provision. Reservations of a general character shall not be permitted under this Article.

(2) Any reservation made under this Article shall contain a brief statement of the law concerned.

ARTICLE 65

(1) A High Contracting Party may denounce the present Convention only after the expiry of five years from the date on which it became a Party to it and after six months' notice contained in a notification addressed to the Secretary-General of the Council of Europe, who shall inform the other High Contracting Parties.

(2) Such a denunciation shall not have the effect of releasing the High Contracting Party concerned from its obligations under this Convention in respect of any act which, being capable of constituting a violation of such obligations, may have been performed by it before the date at which the denunciation became effective.

(3) Any High Contracting Party which shall cease to be a Member of the Council of Europe shall cease to be a Party to this Convention under the same conditions.

(4) The Convention may be denounced in accordance with the provisions of the preceding paragraphs in respect of any territory to which it has been declared to extend under the terms of article 63.

ARTICLE 66

(1) This Convention shall be open to the signature of the Members of the Council of Europe. It shall be ratified. Ratifications shall be deposited with the Secretary-General of the Council of Europe.

(2) The present Convention shall come into force after the deposit of ten instruments of ratification.

(3) As regards any signatory ratifying subsequently, the Convention shall come into force at the date of the deposit of its instrument of ratification.

(4) The Secretary-General of the Council of Europe shall notify all the Members of the Council of Europe of the entry into force of the Convention, the names of the High Contracting Parties who have ratified it, and the deposit of all instruments of ratification which may be effected subsequently.

1990 CHARTER OF PARIS FOR A NEW EUROPE (EXTRACT)

Human Rights, Democracy and Rule of law

We undertake to build, consolidate and strengthen democracy as the only system of government of our nations. In this endeavour, we will abide by the following:

Human rights and fundamental freedoms are the birthright of all human beings, are inalienable and are guaranteed by law. Their protection and promotion is the first responsibility of government. Respect for them is an essential safeguard against an overmighty State. Their observance and full exercise are the foundation of freedom, justice and peace.

Democratic government is based on the will of the people, expressed regularly through free and fair elections. Democracy has as its foundation respect for the human person and the rule of law. Democracy is the best safeguard of freedom of expression, tolerance of all groups of society, and equality of opportunity for each person.

Democracy, with its representative and pluralist character, entails accountability to the electorate, the obligation of public authorities to comply with the law and justice administered impartially. No one will be above the law.

We affirm that, without discrimination,

every individual has the right to:
freedom of thought, conscience and religion or belief,
freedom of expression,
freedom of association and peaceful assembly,
freedom of movement;

no one will be:
subject to arbitrary arrest or detention,
subject to torture or other cruel, inhuman or degrading treatment or punishment;

everyone also has the right:
to know and act upon his rights,

to participate in free and fair elections,
to fair and public trial if charged with an offence,
to own property alone or in association and to exercise individual enterprise,
to enjoy his economic, social and cultural rights.

We affirm that the ethnic, cultural, linguistic and religious identity of national minorities will be protected and that persons belonging to national minorities have the right freely to express, preserve and develop that identity without any discrimination and in full equality before the law.

We will ensure that everyone will enjoy recourse to effective remedies, national or international, against any violation of his rights.

Full respect for these precepts is the bedrock on which we will seek to construct the new Europe.

Our States will co-operate and support each other with the aim of making democratic gains irreversible.

1991 COMMONWEALTH HARARE DECLARATION (EXTRACTS)

... we believe that international peace and order, global economic development and the rule of international law are essential to the security and prosperity of mankind;

we believe in the liberty of the individual under the law, in equal rights for all citizens regardless of gender, race, colour, creed or political belief, and in the individual's inalienable right to participate by means of free and democratic political processes in framing the society in which he or she lives;

we recognise racial prejudice and intolerance as a dangerous sickness and a threat to healthy development, and racial discrimination as an unmitigated evil;

we oppose all forms of racial oppression, and we are committed to the principles of human dignity and equality;

we recognise the importance and urgency of economic and social development to satisfy the basic needs and aspirations of the vast majority of the peoples of the world, and seek the progressive removal of the wide disparities in living standards amongst our members.

Having reaffirmed the principles to which the Commonwealth is committed, and reviewed the problems and challenges which the world, and the Commonwealth as part of it, face, we pledge the Commonwealth and our countries to work with renewed vigour, concentrating especially in the following areas:

the protection and promotion of the fundamental political values of the Commonwealth:

democracy, democratic processes and institutions which reflect national circumstances, the rule of law and the independence of the judiciary, and just and honest government;

fundamental human rights, including equal rights and opportunities for all citizens regardless of race, colour, creed or political belief;

equality for women, so that they may exercise their full and equal rights;

provision of universal access to education for the population of our countries;

continuing action to bring about the end of apartheid and the establishment of a free, democratic, non-racial and prosperous South Africa;

the promotion of sustainable development and the alleviation of poverty in the countries of the Commonwealth through:

a stable international economic framework within which growth can be achieved;

sound economic management recognising the central role of the market economy;

effective population policies and programmes;

sound management of technological change;

the freest possible flow of multilateral trade on terms fair and equitable to all, taking account of the special requirements of developing countries;

an adequate flow of resources from the developed to developing countries, and action to alleviate the debt burdens of developing countries most in need;

the development of human resources, in particular through education, training, health, culture, sport and programmes for strengthening family and community support, paying special attention to the needs of women, youth and children;

effective and increasing programmes of bilateral and multilateral co-operation aimed at raising living standards;

extending the benefits of development within a framework of respect for human rights;

the protection of the environment through respect for the principles of sustainable development which we enunciated at Langkawi;

action to combat drug trafficking and abuse and communicable diseases;

help for small Commonwealth states in tackling their particular economic and security problems;

support of the United Nations and other international institutions in the world's search for peace, disarmament and effective arms control; and in the promotion of international consensus on major global political, economic and social issues.

To give weight and effectiveness to our commitments we intend to focus and improve Commonwealth co-operation in these areas. This would include strengthening the capacity of the Commonwealth to respond to requests from members for assistance in entrenching the practices of democracy, accountable administration and rule of law.

We call on all the intergovernmental institutions of the Commonwealth to seize the opportunities presented by these challenges. We pledge ourselves to assist them to develop programmes which harness our shared historical, professional, cultural and linguistic heritage and which complement the work of other international and regional organisations.

We invite the Commonwealth Parliamentary Association and non-governmental Commonwealth organisations to play their full part in promoting these objectives, in a spirit of co-operation and mutual support.

Further Reading

Annual Reports

Broadcasting Complaints Commission

Broadcasting Standards Council

Commission for Racial Equality

Commissioner of Police of the Metropolis

Criminal Injuries Compensation Board

Crown Office and Procurator Fiscal Service

Crown Prosecution Service

Data Protection Registrar

Employment Service

Equal Opportunities Commission

Equal Opportunities Commission for Northern Ireland

Fair Employment Commission

Health and Safety Executive

Health Service Commissioner

Her Majesty's Chief Inspector of Constabulary

Her Majesty's Chief Inspector of Constabulary for Scotland

Her Majesty's Chief Inspector of Prisons

Parliamentary Commissioner for Administration

Parole Board

Police Complaints Authority

Standing Advisory Commission on Human Rights in Northern Ireland

Other Official Publications

The Citizen's Charter. Cm 1599.	HMSO	1991
Crime, Justice and Protecting the Public. Cm 965.	HMSO	1990
Education and Training for the 21st Century. Cm 1536.	HMSO	1991
Frameworks for the Future.	HMSO	1995
The Future of the BBC: Serving the Nation, Competing World-wide. Cm 2621.	HMSO	1994
One Year On . . . : A Report on the Progress of the Health of the Nation. Department of Health.	HMSO	1993
Open Government. Cm 2290.	HMSO	1993
Police and Criminal Evidence Act 1984 (s66) Codes of Practice.	HMSO	1986
Privacy and Media Intrusion: The Government's Response. Cm 2918.	HMSO	1995
Report of the Committee on Privacy and Related Matters. Cm 1102.	HMSO	1990
Report of the Royal Commission on Criminal Justice.	HMSO	1993
Royal Commission on Criminal Justice. Interim Government Response.	HMSO	1994
Scotland's Children: Proposals for Child Care Policy and Law. Cm 2286.	HMSO	1993
Security, Equality, Choice: The Future for Pensions. Cm 2594-1.	HMSO	1994

The Sentence of the Court: A Handbook for Courts
on the Treatment of Offenders.   HMSO   1994

Women and Men in Britain.
                    Equal Opportunities Commission   1994

Index

arrests and criminal proceedings 25–6
police powers 26
warrants in Scotland 26
arrested people, rights of 26–8
bail 29–30
charging 29
codes of practice 26–7
Criminal Justice and Public Order Act 1994 and 'right to silence' 27
detention and writ of habeas corpus 28
detention time in Scotland 28
Director of Public Prosecutions (Northern Ireland) 31
interviews, tape recording of 28
police caution 27, 29
police powers and non-intimate body samples 28
prosecution 30–1
public prosecutors (Scotland) 31
'right to silence' legislation (Northern Ireland) 27
solicitors 27
suspects and detention time 27–8
time limits on remands in custody 30
See also Crown Prosecution Service and prosecution; Crown Prosecutors; magistrates' courts
assemblies and associations (Article 20) 58–9
police powers relating to 59
asylum (Article 14) 42–5

Asylum and Immigration Appeals Act 1993 43–4
asylum seekers 43
Dublin Convention 44
extradition and British policy 44–5
United Nations Convention Relating to the Status of Refugees 1951 (and 1967 Protocol) 43

Bill of Rights 1689 12
British Government 2, 3
broadcasting 54–7
broadcasting by cable and satellite channels 57
broadcasting companies 56
Broadcasting Complaints Commission 55
Broadcasting Standards Council 55
codes of practice 55
parliamentary and political broadcasting 56
programme standards in broadcasting 55–6
violence and obscenity in 55

Charter of Paris for a New Europe text (extract) 162–3
Commission for Racial Equality 15–16
codes of practice 16
Commonwealth, the 9–10
Commonwealth Harare Declaration (1991) 9
Secretariat 9–10

text (extract) 164–6
Conference on Security and
  Co-operation in Europe 8
Council of Europe 2, 5–6, 9, 40, 44
  Committee of Ministers 7
  Convention on the Transfer of
    Sentenced Persons 22
courts and media reporting 33–4
  protection of children 33
  rape cases 33
  restriction on reporting 34
Criminal Justice Act 1991 20, 21
criminal trials (Article 11) 34–7
  appeals 36–7
  rights of the defence 35–6
  rules of evidence 36
  sentencing 37
  See also Independent Criminal
    Cases Review Commission; Royal
    Commission on Criminal Justice
Crown Prosecution Service and
  prosecution 30–1
Crown Prosecutors 30–1

data protection 40–1
  computers and privacy 40–1
  Council of Europe convention 40
  Data Protection Act 1989 40
  national security and 41
  Office of the Data Protection
    Registrar 41
detention, unlawful or arbitrary 11
discrimination 13
  European Community legislation
    14–15

early release (remission) of prisoners
  21
  Northern Ireland 21
education: government policy 88–9
education: schools 89–95
  Celtic languages 93–4

ethnic minorities 94–5
rights of parents 89–90
school curriculum 91–3
special educational needs 94
education: post-school education
  95–7
further education colleges 96
grants and loans 95–6
Open University 96
schools 97
education, science and the arts
  (Articles 26–7) 88–101
arts, the 98–9
British Council 100
copyright and patents 100–1
EUREKA scheme 100
European Union science and
  research programmes 100
Office of Science and Technology
  99–100
research on science and technology
  99–100
equality before the law 23–31
  (Articles 6–9)
equal opportunities (Article 2) 13–17
discrimination 13
Equal Opportunities Commission 14
Equal Opportunities Commission for
  Northern Ireland 14
equal pay 14
  See also social rights: pay and
    working conditions
European Commission of Human
  Rights 6–7
European Convention for the
  Protection of Human Rights and
    Fundamental Freedoms 5–7
British Government and 7
enforcement 6–7
Protocols 6
restrictions 6
text 144–61

United Kingdom immigration
control system and 6
European Convention on the
Suppression of Terrorism 44
European Court of Human Rights 7
European Union 2, 9, 11–12, 44
Council 63
European Commission 63
European Parliament 63–4

firearms 7
freedom of expression (Article 19)
53–8
defamation 53–4
films and video 58
official information 53
press 54
restriction on court reporting 53
theatre 57–8
See also broadcasting
freedom of movement (Article 13)
41–2
detention or restriction and 42
freedom of choice of residence 42
police powers to stop and search
42
requirement to produce passport or
travel document 42

habeas corpus *see* detention, unlawful
or arbitrary; arrested people: detention and writ of habeas
corpus
Helsinki Final Act (1975) 8
housing 84–8
homeless people 86–7
home renovation grants 88
housing action trusts 86
housing associations 85–6
privately rented housing 87
public sector housing 84–5

Independent Criminal Cases Review
Commission 36–7
interception of communications
39–40
International Covenant on Civil and
Political Rights 4–5
derogations from 4–5
implementation 5
Optional Protocol 5
text of Optional Protocol 139–43
text 116–38
International Covenant on Economic,
Social and Cultural Rights 3–5
text 103–15

judicial control of public authorities
24

legal aid 23–4, 49
Citizens Advice Bureaux 24
legal procedure (Articles 10–11) 31–7
abolition of trial by jury (Northern
Ireland) 32
administrative tribunals 34
Council on Tribunals 34
courts 31–2
Crown Courts 32
district courts (Scotland) 31–2
High Court of Judiciary (Scotland)
32
judiciary 31
jury and jurors 32–3
lay magistrates' courts 31
sheriff court (Scotland) 32
tax tribunals 34
See also criminal trials
legal redress and remedies 23
Welsh language and 23
life sentence prisoners 22

magistrates' courts 31
maladministration 24–5

codes of practice on open
government 25
complaints and remedies 24
local government and the National
Health Service 25
Lord Chancellor's Department 24
Northern Ireland's Complaints
Commissioner 25
Parliamentary Ombudsman 24
marriage and the family (Article 16)
47–50
children 49
family 48
Hague convention 49
marriage 47
succession rights 49–50

National Health Service 73–81
adoption 79–80
children in care 77–9
dental services 74
eye care 74–5
families and children 76–7
family doctors 73–4
hospital services 75
personal social services 76
private medical care 75–6
social security 80–1
See also political rights: Citizen's
Charter
nationality (Article 15) 45–7
British Nationality Act 1981 45
citizenships, forms of 45–6
legislation on Falkland Island and
Hong Kong citizens 47
residence requirements, marriage
and 46
non-custodial treatment 20–1
compulsory community service 21
probation 21
Northern Ireland 16–17, 62–3
Anglo-Irish Agreement (1985) 62

Fair Employment Commission 16
Fair Employment Tribunal 16
Frameworks for the Future
document 63
Joint Declaration (1993) 62–3
religious composition of workforces
16
Standing Advisory Committee on
Human Rights 17

Organisation for Security and
Co-operation in Europe 2, 8

Parliament 11–12
Parliamentary Ombudsman 24
parole 21–2
Criminal Justice Act 1991 20
Parole Board 22
Passport Office 42
Police, complaints against 25
political asylum *see* asylum
political rights (Article 21) 59–66
Citizen's Charter 64–6
elections 60–2
open government 66
Parliament 60
public service 64
voting rights 60–1
See also European Union:
European Parliament;
Northern Ireland
press and privacy 38–9
code of practice 38
Press Complaints Commission 38
press standards 38
Privacy and Media Intrusion
government White Paper 39
voluntary regulation 38–9
privacy, right to (Article 12) 37–41
intrusion (bugging, criminal
trespass, harassment of tenants,
unsolicited obscene material) 39

law and 37–8
libel 39
See also interception of communications; press and privacy
property (Article 17) 50
protection of the person (Articles 3–5) 17–22
protection for accused people 20
codes of practice 20

racial equality 15
racial hatred, incitement to 19
religious toleration (Article 18) 50–3
blasphemous libel 51
Churches of England and Scotland 2
religions in Britain 51–2
religious education in schools 52
television and radio 53
remission *see* early release of prisoners
Royal Commission on Criminal Justice 37

sex discrimination 13–14
complaints and remedies 14
education and training 14
industrial tribunals and employment 14
slavery (Article 4) 19–20
social rights (Articles 22–5) 66–88
abortion 83
equal pay and opportunities 69
health 73–81
health and safety 70–1
help to unemployed people 76–8
hours of work and holidays 72–3

human fertilisation and embryology 83–4
mothers and children 81–3
pay and working conditions 69–70
surrogacy 84
trade unions 71–2
training 68
See also housing; National Health Service

taking of life 17
terrorism, measures against 18–19
anti-terrorism legislation 19
British Government and 19
emergency legislation and powers (Northern Ireland) 18–19

United Nations 1, 2, 3–5, 44
UN Charter 3
UN Economic and Social Council 4
UN Universal Declaration on Human Rights 1, 3, 5, 13
See also individual articles
UN World Conference on Human Rights 2
use of custody 20
Criminal Justice Act 1991 20

violence to the person 17–18
compensation 18
Criminal Injuries Compensation Scheme 18
Victim Support 18
witness service 18

Printed in the United Kingdom for HMSO.
Dd.301816, 2/96, C30, 56–6734, 5673, 339461.